Praise for *Protect Your Purse*

Doris Belland relies heavily on her own story and those of other women she knows to help you find your financial path without relying too much on a spouse or partner. Being widowed at 32 and having to repay a mound of debt helps her teach lessons she's learned at great personal expense. I found the book a quick and entertaining read, full of practical tips to help you get started and stay on track.

— Ellen Roseman, Toronto Star consumer columnist, personal finance speaker and instructor at University of Toronto school of continuing studies.

Once I entered into Doris's world, I quickly came to the conclusion that *Protect your Purse* is a book that all parents will want to share with their children, both male and female, as part of their life skills learning. And all women will want to share this book with their girlfriends.

She has shared financial strengthening tools that are easy to fit into our day-to-day life. Her book helps us all to remember that we, too, are worth it and we need to keep asking questions.

— Jacqueline Hunter, CLU, CHS, Financial Advisor/Owner, The Co-Operators

I've been in finance for twenty years and have seen countless situations where clients would have been well-served by a little hindsight. Doris has seen her fair share of what life can throw at you. She writes with honesty, humor and style to help us handle the ever-shifting landscape of life. The advice, tips and stories serve as an important reminder for us all to be better prepared. It's imperative. Read this book!

— Sandra Tisiot, Mortgage Professional, Creator MyLifeLocker, Founder WomenInBusinessConference.ca

I've met many business women throughout my life and I can attest with confidence that Doris is, by far, the smartest and most practical woman I know about finance and investing. I am astounded by the clarity she brings to complex issues around family and finance, and she offers practical and actionable advice you can bank on. I will refer her book to all the women in my life.

— Nick Legault
CEO of Building Investments Inc

This book puts into perspective how quickly your world can change. Although my wife and I (or maybe it was just I) thought we had everything absolutely squared away with respect to finances, wills and insurance, Doris's book sparked some discussion on "what if?" And surprisingly, we were not on the same page in all cases. We are now.

Protect Your Purse will help a lot of husbands, like me, who want to do the right thing, but perhaps, don't really want to think about it.

— Robi Khan, Director of Analytics, Kinaxis

PROTECT
YOUR
PURSE

PROTECT YOUR PURSE

Shared Lessons for Women:
Avoid Financial Messes, Stop Emotional Bankruptcies,
and Take Charge of Your Money

—————— DORIS BELLAND ——————

DORIS BELLAND
Survive, Thrive and Grow

Protect Your Purse—Shared Lessons for Women: Avoid Financial Messes, Stop Emotional Bankruptcies, and Take Charge of Your Money

For information about this title or to order other books and/or electronic media, contact the author:

Doris Belland
http://dorisbelland.com
doris@dorisbelland.com

Published in Canada by Felicis Press

ISBNs:
Print: 978-0-9958218-0-4
eBook: 978-0-9958218-1-1

Editor: Kimberly Rempel
Cover and Interior design: 1106 Design

For Ron, Andrea, and Jeff, who carried me through the hardest year.

For Mark, who believed before I did.

For Malcolm, who started it all.

They who have sympathy and imagination to make the sorrows of others their own can readily learn all the hard lessons of life from the experience of others.

— Elizabeth Cady Stanton

Say something that no other person could possibly say.

— Lawrence Hill

CONTENTS

PART I – *Experience*   1

PART II – *Lessons*   45

PREFACE

I remember the morning of November 22nd, 2000, clearly. It was the second time my life took a drastic turn. The sun shone through my living room windows, and outside even the leafless trees looked cheerful. Despite the sun and warmth of the morning, my mood was low.

I sat on the staircase adjacent to the living room, staring outside. All I could think about was the mess my life was still in. My late husband Malcolm had been gone for two years, and, while I had made a conscious decision to move on, I was no longer quite sure of what that meant. Whatever it meant to move forward, I was pretty certain I was failing.

A new man, Mark, had just entered my life, and, as much as I paid lip service to being ready for a new relationship, my feelings betrayed uncertainty. When you spend nearly ten years with someone you love and then suddenly he's gone, it's immensely difficult to begin again. Frankly, it's just plain strange to have another man in your house, in your life, and in your space when most of your memory is insisting that space belongs to someone else.

That morning in November I was thinking about the impossibility of this new relationship and of the many unknowns I faced. What the hell was I doing?

I was originally going to wind down my wholesale-retail business, which was really Malcolm's business, sell the house, and travel for a year to regain my footing. I had no idea what I would do afterward—that was a whole other problem.

Now there was Mark, a guy who had just come back from a year of travel and who was ready to settle down into his career and a family life of his own, a trajectory that didn't fit with my plans at all.

There was also the issue of money. At that point I had repaid the business debt left behind when Malcolm died, and I had renovated the house to a point where it could be sold. With the sale of the house, I would be left with a bit of money. It would be enough to travel for a year but not much beyond that. The frustrating part was that I had just climbed out of debt only to find myself back at zero with a big question mark for a future.

How would I earn a living after that? For heaven's sake, I was 34. It was inconceivable to me to be so rudderless in my mid-thirties. Me. Directionless. It was absurd. So much of my life had been charted and mapped out carefully, including university, scholarships, even a doctorate. I'd had a plan and was on track, or at least I had been on track until Malcolm got sick. Then my life derailed.

What had happened to all that careful planning? How could I have gotten myself into this situation? Had I been dumb or naïve? How was it possible to end up in such a weak, vulnerable position? My head hurt just thinking about it.

There were still four weeks left in the Christmas retail season, and I was working sixteen-hour days, six days a week, to sell off as much business inventory as possible before closing the doors for good. I was depleted physically and emotionally. It had been a long two years.

And on top of it all, now there was Mark. He had just travelled; I hadn't escaped yet. He wanted to get serious; I couldn't imagine anything of the kind. He was happy and optimistic; I was mending and still cynical about my future. It couldn't possibly work. Plus, he was so different from Malcolm.

I sat on the stairs, head in hands, shoulders slumped, unable to imagine what was next for me and unsure where to start. Everything looked and felt impossible. The more I tried to figure it out, the more impenetrable my situation appeared. More than anything, I was tired.

Then something surprising happened. Mark settled down on the stair behind me and wrapped his arms around my shoulders. I was so lost in thought I hadn't even heard him approaching.

"What are you thinking?" he asked.

"About everything I have to do. There's so much, I don't even know where to start."

"It will all work out."

I tried to smile. Poor guy, he really had no clue. Blind optimism, meet your poster boy.

"It *will*. I'll help."

There was no drama in his voice. He said it matter-of-factly, as though certain of the outcome.

I stared at him. As I thought about how to explain my reality to him, something shifted in me. I don't know why it happened or what triggered it, but I felt a visceral calm start to take root. This wasn't a dramatic moment; it was more of a gradual shift in my attitude. The longer I sat, the more I felt something akin to internal walls starting to cave. A belief kicked in, a knowing that reaches far beyond the limitations of the rational mind.

For the first time since Malcolm's death, I started to believe a good future might just be possible. I finally understood there were people who would help if I'd let them.

I have no idea why I didn't just cynically dismiss Mark's optimism, but I didn't. In that moment, I believed him.

Mark was right. It did work out.

My life today would be unrecognizable to my thirty-year-old self. I have remarried, something I never thought I'd do, mostly because I didn't think it was possible to love someone other than Malcolm. I have two daughters—also unimaginable. We live in a lovely house and are surrounded by a large group of supportive friends. I have built a successful local business and am now growing an international business that supports women. The only debt I have is productive debt for real estate assets I have steadily acquired over the past decade.

In the days after Malcolm's death or at any point beforehand, if you had told me this would be my reality, I would have dismissed you as mad.

Yet here I am.

Ever since Malcolm's death more than a decade ago, I've been thinking about how I can help women avoid the mistakes I made. For the longest time I resisted sharing anything at all, questioning the value of my experiences.

What if my case was really a one-off? What if the circumstances of my story were so unique they didn't resonate with anyone else? Would the lessons I learned ever make a difference for someone else? Plus, who wants to publicly admit they made a lot of really naive mistakes? Then there was the perennial question of "Who really cares?" Does the world need yet another book about some poor woman's sob story? What would that accomplish?

The idea wouldn't go away. Mark kept urging me to start a blog.

"What would I write about?" I asked.

"Talk to people about all of the things you've told me. Share your experiences."

In March of 2012, I began to wake up at 5am with paragraphs running through my mind. Complete essays formed themselves while

I tried to ignore them and go back to sleep. When this happened seven days in a row, I gave in and finally sat down to record the essays. That's when it dawned on me. I had the beginning of a blog. Mark put together a rudimentary site for me, and I started to share my thoughts publicly. To my surprise, people started to read and comment.

I reached out to a few widows and divorcees to interview them about their own experiences. I wanted to know once and for all if there was any overlap in the challenges we faced and the lessons we learned. Were we all just single data points in our individual stories, or were we part of a bigger, more predictable picture? If there were common experiences, what were they?

Word spread. Other widows and divorcees contacted me to share their stories. In the end, I spoke with more than three dozen women and captured a few of their stories on my blog.

I had originally suspected there would be some common ground, but the extent to which we faced similar challenges took me aback. It turns out that loss of any kind, whether through death or divorce, leaves most women facing the same sorts of issues.

I continued to share my thoughts and a few of the women's stories on the blog. One day Mark asked me how many people were reading the posts. I was stunned to discover my posts were being read by people in more than thirty-five countries. I don't even know people in thirty-five countries! That was the first real sign that my message resonated beyond my family and friends.

It was time to get serious about writing the book that had been lingering inside me for more than a decade. This book is a small part of my story and a compilation of the lessons I've learned since Malcolm's death. It's all the stuff I wish someone had told me as I started to define my life and make choices that would have unexpected consequences down the road.

You may think that because I was a widow, this book is for widows. It's not. Nor is it aimed at divorcees, whose experiences often mirror that of widows. This book is for *all* women.

I wish one of my trusted mentors had sat me down many years ago and said something like this:

"Listen, there are things you need to know and a lot of financial changes you need to make. I know you think you're fine and smart and on top of it. Many women think they're fine and they will always be fine.

"However, at some point you will encounter difficult moments. They will test you. They may even change your life. Prepare for them.

"And please don't tell me that you're too busy. That's rubbish. You make time for the things that matter most.

"What I'm about to tell you matters even if you're married to the nicest guy on the planet and he lives to be a hundred years old. It matters even if you both have terrific jobs or businesses that will sustain you into the sunset.

"This will be critical when something rotten happens. And it will."

One of the first things that occurred to me after Malcolm's death was that I wanted my life to serve a purpose. I wanted to be useful. I wasn't sure how I was going to manage it, but I set it as an overriding goal. This project is part of that quest.

I sincerely hope you find this book useful in some way. If you do, please share it with other women in your life.

Doris Belland
Ottawa, Ontario
Canada

PART I

Experience

RED RIBBONS

I am not a product of my circumstances.
I am a product of my decisions.

— Stephen R. Covey

D o you remember the first time you desperately wanted something? I do. It was on Track-and-Field day in grade six. Earlier that year I had graduated from elementary school to middle school—or junior high school as it was called in Alberta back then—which meant I was now in the big leagues. Finally I was part of the all-important group of older kids.

Track-and-Field day provided participants with one key attraction: we got to miss a whole day of school in order to compete in a wide variety of events. Don't get me wrong: I enjoyed school, but seriously, who wouldn't want to skip six hours of sitting in a concrete box to run around outside on a beautiful spring day?

The school field had been transformed into an official-looking track with white paint delineating lanes, ovals, and starting points. Some of the teachers had stopwatches hanging from their necks, and others carried clipboards to record results. (Now you know how old I am given the tools of the sporting trade back then.)

I participated in four or five events that day, but all I walked away with was a fourth-place ribbon for shot put. As I stared at other students walking around with red first-place ribbons pinned to their shirts, I longed to have one of my own. I looked around at my competition. I knew if I wanted to make it to first place, I'd have to get serious about practicing.

So I did. I started running every day. On weekends I would sign out a discus and a shot from the gym, and then I'd head to the field-sized lawn on our farm to figure out how to hold and throw the things. I sought books about great athletes to see what they did to excel. This was long before the Internet, which meant there were few resources beyond the town's tiny library. I had a handful of dated books to refer to, and that was it.

All the athletes in those books seemed to be muscular, so I started doing push ups, sit ups, and other drills I imagined would get the job done. I ran miles and miles on the country roads beside our farm. I'd run in the rain, in blazing hot sun, and on cold days when I could see my breath. If the road was passable, I was on it. I'd run through the grassy fields and up and down the hills behind our house, dodging cow manure and gopher holes. The whole time I imagined myself crossing the finish line in a blaze of glory, arms raised in victory.

It was all fairly corny, but it did the trick. My enthusiastic yet entirely uneducated stab at training pushed me far enough forward that I started winning. In grade seven, I reached my goal of having a couple red ribbons on my shirt. By grade nine, I won all of my events.

Let's put this into perspective. This was in northern Alberta against other untrained kids in an area with low population density. This fish had succeeded in a tiny pond. There were no accolades or scholarships, just shiny ribbons to take home and pin in an album. It was not a big deal really. . . . Except it was for me.

What I learned through the process is this: if you have a goal and work tirelessly on it every single day, persisting through obstacles, you will eventually succeed. That lesson stayed with me through my adolescence and into my early twenties.

I would set goals, work hard, and achieve them. I would set new goals, get back to work, and continue to move forward. The path certainly wasn't linear; there were setbacks and big disappointments just as there are for everyone else. Most of the time when I failed, I would get frustrated, feel sorry for myself for a bit, blame everything and anything for the failure (including myself), and then get back to work with even more determination.

> IF YOU HAVE A GOAL AND WORK TIRELESSLY ON IT EVERY SINGLE DAY, PERSISTING THROUGH OBSTACLES, YOU WILL EVENTUALLY SUCCEED.

This approach got me through high school, an undergraduate degree via two universities, a year-long scholarship in France, and post-graduate work.

Then, in my twenties, something went terribly wrong: I discovered that every rule has an exception. For me, Malcolm was the exception.

MALCOLM

... The most important thing about any person is what you don't know. Likewise, then, the most important part of any story is the missing piece.

— Barbara Kingsolver, *The Lacuna*

I couldn't believe his nerve.

A girlfriend and I were enjoying a pint at a campus pub in celebration of a successful day at our university's Model United Nations. As the representatives for Jordan and France, respectively, we felt our efforts called for a toast. It didn't hurt that my friend was keen on one of the bartenders at the pub. We parked ourselves at the bar and proceeded to chat with other students.

It was all quite pleasant until a guy with long hair, torn jeans, construction boots, and a beaten leather satchel walked up to the bar. Given the way he was greeted by the staff and other patrons, he was clearly well-known and liked.

As soon as he started to speak, though, I couldn't figure out why people seemed to like him so much. Sure, he was devastatingly funny, but it was often at someone else's expense. From the moment he arrived, he took center stage and proceeded to rant about everything. He tore verbal strips off a few people, including my friend. Some took it in stride and exchanged sarcastic barbs with him, while others just smiled and let him get away with it. I was shocked that my friend wasn't saying anything, particularly since she didn't know the guy. Why on earth were people putting up with his crap?

To my astonishment, he decided to have a go at me. Here he was, a perfect stranger, trying to verbally joust with me. What the hell? Maybe that kind of garbage worked with others, but I wouldn't have any of it. I stopped him in his tracks, told him exactly what I thought of his antics in reasonably uncomplimentary terms, and walked out of the pub.

The next afternoon, just as I was getting back from a class, one of my housemates told me there was a message for me from some guy named Malcolm.

"Malcolm? I don't know anyone named Malcolm. Are you sure the name's right?"

I racked my brain. Who on earth was Malcolm? I'd never met anyone named Malcolm.

Then the light went on: he was the jerk from the pub. And now he was calling me? Maybe he was phoning to apologize. I couldn't imagine why else he would call, given how he had behaved and what I'd said to him. I figured I'd give the guy a chance to make amends. We all make mistakes—right?

"I was calling to see if you'd like to go out for coffee."

And this is where I wondered if the guy was brain damaged. I couldn't believe he had just asked me out.

"Are you kidding me?"

"You told me to fuck off. No one has ever done that to me. I want to see you again."

"You were an ass and now you want me to go out for coffee with you?"

"Yes, I know. I didn't mean it. Now will you have coffee with me?"

"You can't be serious. No, I will not have coffee with you."

"I'm perfectly serious. Will you join me for coffee? Better yet, how about a drink at the pub tonight?"

"First you behave like a jerk, then you're intrigued because I told you to fuck off, which is precisely what you deserved, by the way. Not much of a selling point. Is this how you typically approach women? Because it won't work with me."

This went on for a bit, but he was persistent. Honestly, I don't know what possessed me to agree. I should have hung up the phone, chalked up the experience to yet another example of bad behavior by a university guy, and moved on. Perhaps I was curious to see what he was really like, or maybe I'm the one who was brain damaged. In any case, I eventually said yes.

To my dismay we hit it off. I really wanted to dislike the guy, to be mad at him, and to prove he really was a jerk. I wanted my initial assessment to be correct. However, I had never laughed as hard in my life as I did that night. I had dated bright, clever men before but none like him. This guy had a high level of intelligence, razor-sharp wit, political awareness, literary knowledge, love of the outdoors, intellectual curiosity, and musical ability—he had it all.

Malcolm was, and remains to this day, the most devastatingly funny man I had ever met. In so many respects we were polar opposites: the way we dressed, our life paths, our backgrounds, our families, our goals, and our approach to education and money. Yet no one had ever engaged me intellectually like he did. He was fun, charismatic, unpredictable, and hilarious—the good boy and the bad boy all rolled up into one.

Despite my better judgment, I was hooked.

On the second day of our courtship, Malcolm sat me down and told me he had something important to say.

"Sounds dramatic."

He wasn't smiling. He held up a Budweiser cap that he had hammered into a ring, which immediately made me think, "You drink that crap?" Before I could say anything, he started.

"I think I want to marry you." He must have seen my eyes double in size because he put up his hand and urged me to listen. "There's something you need to know. I have cancer; Hodgkin's disease. I've had it since I was five, but they only diagnosed it when I was thirteen. By then it had spread everywhere, and the doctors didn't expect me to make it to my eighteenth birthday. Here I am at twenty-two. I'm in remission, but who knows how long it will last? My doctors aren't optimistic. I'm telling you this because I want to give you the chance to walk away before you break my heart. I'll understand if you want to leave."

I'm quite certain if you had punched me in the face at that moment, I wouldn't have felt it. I just sat there, stunned. Which was crazier: that a guy I'd known barely one week just talked to me about marriage, with a Budweiser cap for an engagement ring no less, or that he had been dealing with cancer since he was a child? It was overwhelming. For once I was speechless. When I eventually found my voice again, all I could say was, "That's crazy."

He shrugged. "That's what you get with me."

There was no pathos in his voice, just resignation. He had been living with cancer for a long time and had become accustomed to letting go of hopes and aspirations. For him, there would be no children; the treatments had taken care of that. Nor did he believe a woman would stay when she discovered his reality.

Before meeting me, he had garnered a reputation for being a bit of a Casanova. "Love them and leave them before things get serious" appeared to be his motto. When I first met his father, Ron, who would later become one of the dearest people in my life, he made it clear he didn't think I would last.

"Malcolm doesn't have long-term relationships. You won't last."

"He'll be lucky if he lasts in my world." I shot back, "He's the one pursuing me, not the other way around."

"We'll see how long that lasts," replied Ron. He later apologized to me for that exchange. "You're not like the others. Malcolm is genuinely in love with you," he admitted.

I conceded, "Malcolm isn't like the others, either."

Call it optimism or delusion, I'm not sure which it was, but I stayed. In my limited experience at the time, I believed every problem could be solved by research, a plan, and hard work. I figured this would be no different. It sounds naive in retrospect, but I really did believe we could beat the cancer. We would research the best diet, optimize his current good health, and everything would eventually work out. I certainly didn't think it would be easy, just doable.

I told Malcolm I was not prepared to commit to anything serious on day two, but I did tell him cancer wasn't going to scare me away. I suggested we continue to enjoy each other's company and see what happens.

Six months later, the cancer was back.

ALWAYS CANCER

Never, never, never give up.

— WINSTON CHURCHILL

My first experience with oncology was sitting with Malcolm in his doctor's office when he was told the biopsy from a lymph node in his neck was positive. The guy had been through this so often he pretty much expected it. I however, was devastated and petrified.

To me, cancer had only ever struck others. Sure, I had heard of people who'd had the disease, many of whom died from it, but it had never struck so close to home. This time it was personal. My illusions of helping Malcolm to grow ever-healthier were shaken.

Malcolm was wonderful during that first stressful period. He had been through this a million times and understood how much of a shock it all was to me. We spent a lot of time hiking in the woods and sitting at a nearby lake, talking it through. We fed each other's sense of optimism and determination. We would get through this and do whatever it took to succeed.

Anyone who has been through cancer treatments knows how awful they are, particularly the treatments available during the 1980s and 1990s. Looking back, some of the standard medications from that time seem terribly barbaric by today's standards. Nausea, indigestion, immunity issues, overwhelming fatigue, and sores of all kinds were just some of the side effects of the treatments Malcolm endured.

It took me a long time to realize the extent to which Malcolm minimized any negative physical impact on himself. The world around him never really knew how much pain he endured. Even I was sheltered from the full truth. His stoicism was remarkable.

The first in a long line of treatments began shortly after we got the news. It began with radiation. That wasn't so bad, all things considered. It tired Malcolm out and affected certain parts of his body, but he could still function reasonably well. When the treatment was done, he seemed to be getting better.

During that time I completed my undergraduate degree at Queen's University and moved to Montreal to work on my Master's degree at McGill University. Given Malcolm's dependence on his oncology team, there was no way that he was going to move out of Kingston, so he stayed behind and started a screen-printing business that made good use of his artistic abilities.

Every Thursday night he would drive to Montreal to spend an extended weekend with me, returning to Kingston after dinner on Sunday. It wasn't ideal, but we both knew it was temporary. I would finish my studies, and we'd be together after that.

In May of 1991, two years after we met, we eloped with only a handful of close friends present at the ceremony. There were no family members for two primary reasons: first, Malcolm's parents were dead set against our marriage. Ron still thought Malcolm wasn't capable of long-term commitment given his past, and his mom felt we weren't financially ready for marriage. After all, she argued, Malcolm had just started a business, and I was still a student. Privately, she also told me I didn't know what I was getting into. While she never came out and said it directly, the implication was that it wasn't wise to get involved with someone who has cancer. That approach didn't help my already-strained relationship with her.

Second, my family all lived several provinces away, and we simply couldn't afford to do anything formal for them. When you're related to a good chunk of a province as I am—there are ten children in each of my parents' families—where do you draw the line? The more we thought about it, the more stressed we became until we decided to chuck all thoughts of a traditional marriage out the window and elope instead.

In the end, we disclosed our intentions to ten friends, who all pitched in to make it a special day. We were married on Queen's campus by the university chaplain, and the celebration afterwards consisted of a potluck dinner provided by our friends at a parents' house along the waterfront. The next morning we left for a last-minute, dirt-cheap vacation in Costa Rica, where we spent a magical week pretending we didn't have a care in the world. There were no thoughts of cancer or business or studies or financial stress, only the joy of discovering tropical rain forests, locally grown coffee, and some of the most beautiful beaches I have ever seen.

By 1992 things were looking up. After the first year of my Master's degree, I was promoted to the doctoral program and won a scholarship that would allow me to focus solely on my research. Meanwhile, Malcolm had launched a series of his own designs on t-shirts that had taken off in the marketplace. On a whim, he decided to participate in a retail fair at a nearby university, where he made $12,000 in three days selling shirts. Unfortunately, he had printed only enough stock for $4,000 of sales, a number which had seemed outrageous to him at the time. It never occurred to either of us that it was possible to sell three times that number of t-shirts in a few days.

When the sale closed down after the first day, and for both nights after that, Malcolm drove back to Kingston, four hours away, to print more stock for the next day's sales. His was such a rudimentary operation that he could not accept credit cards, only cash. At the end of the three days, he had a plastic bag full of cash and virtually no shirts left.

After that weekend, Malcolm abandoned the commercial screen printing side of his business and turned his attention to the popular new line of designs, while I concentrated on my doctoral thesis. During the week we lived our separate lives in our respective cities, and on weekends he would drive up to stay with me. Neither of us complained; we were both successful, and we knew the separation wouldn't last forever.

On one of his visits to Montreal, we decided to go for lunch at a nearby restaurant. We parked the car across the street, and I walked to the other side, thinking Malcolm was right beside me. When I got to the restaurant door, I realized I hadn't seen him. I turned and found him on his knees in the middle of the road. Traffic had stopped behind him. I ran and helped him get back on his feet. With one arm around me, he limped to the sidewalk.

"What on earth happened?"

"My legs gave out; they just stopped working, and I collapsed. I couldn't make them move for a few seconds. They still feel shaky. I don't know what's going on."

I took Malcolm back to our car and drove him straight to the cancer clinic in Kingston, two hours away, where his oncologist immediately put him through a battery of tests. I tried to distract myself with books, magazines, and pretty much anything I could get my hands on while we waited for the results, but it didn't work. I was worried sick and so was Malcolm. In his usual, stoic way, he tried to make light of it all, but I wasn't having any of it. I knew this was serious.

I will never forget the look on the doctor's face when he walked back into his office to give us the news.

"There's no easy way to say this. There's a tumor wrapped around your spine."

The tumor had compressed his spine, causing the temporary paralysis. Our choices were bleak. We could either do nothing and face certain paralysis or undergo major surgery to try to remove the tumor. The risk of paralysis was still high given the nature of the surgery, but there was a chance they could remove it without damaging the spinal cord. There were no guarantees that they could remove it all, however.

I can't remember how long that surgery took but I do know it felt like an eternity. Malcolm's father, Ron, and I paced the hallways of the hospital, staring anxiously at anyone who came through the surgical doors. Ron was normally jovial with me, but that day neither of us said anything. We walked, we sat, we waited, we hoped.

When they finally wheeled Malcolm in from recovery, he looked at us groggily and said with his characteristic impish grin, "I can move my toes!" That's the first time that I remember crying in front of Malcolm. I had always tried to hold it together in the past, but that day relief and gratitude overwhelmed me. He was not paralyzed!

We later learned from the surgeon that he had removed most if not all of the tumor. Time would tell, but for now we had the best news possible. The recovery would be long, and there would, of course, be treatments, but we could move forward.

The first days passed by in a blur. All I thought about was Malcolm's physical recovery and the logistics of his medical appointments. It took a few weeks for the reality of my own situation to fully sink in. While my thesis supervisor had been understanding, giving me all the time I needed to deal with Malcolm's urgent medical issues, I started to feel the pressure of time passing. Thankfully it was summer, and there weren't any students around, which meant I didn't have any duties as a teaching assistant. Still, I was keenly aware my research had stalled. I owed my supervisor a call to discuss the next steps. The only problem was that I had no clue what the next steps would be.

How could I go back to Montreal when my husband was recovering from surgery and undergoing cancer treatments? It was true he was making rapid progress, but he was still weak and needed a lot of help. We weren't talking about a matter of weeks here; we were talking months of treatments and recovery. No one could say for certain how long it would take to get him back on his feet and functioning normally. And what about his business? Malcolm was feeling a lot of stress about that, and stress, as we well knew, was the enemy. We had to find a way to reduce it at all costs.

I could help Malcolm while continuing my studies if he were in Montreal, but I knew he wouldn't leave his comfort zone in Kingston. His doctors had been with him since he was a young child. The idea of moving to a new city and transferring to a new team in a new hospital was a non-starter. On the other hand, the research for my PhD in neurolinguistics could not be done in Kingston. This was in the early 1990s, and the Internet as we know it today was not yet developed. My physical presence was required both for classes and for a large part of the work I needed to do.

I eventually called my thesis supervisor to request a one-year leave of absence. I had talked myself into believing that Malcolm should be better within one year and then I could resume my research. I would continue the research as I could while in Kingston but would formally restart my studies the following year. We requested, and were granted, a one-year leave from the issuer of the scholarship. While this arrangement wasn't ideal, at least all was not lost.

Malcolm did not get well. He recovered from the surgery, but his cancer never left him for long. He would have a period of relatively good health, and then the cancer would flare up again. There was not a single year from 1992 until his death in 1998 in which he did not undergo some form of cancer treatment.

After a few years of recurrences, his doctors suggested his only hope was an autologous bone-marrow transplant. The only problem was, given his thick file (actually, he had multiple files by the time he was in his mid-twenties), he was not a great candidate. His doctors went to bat for him, doing what they could to get him on the list for the procedure. At one point it looked like the whole process would be derailed when our medical system refused to cover the cost of the drugs involved. There was no way we could afford to pay for thousands of dollars of medications. By some fluke, Malcolm was present when the drug representative was in the hospital, and they ended up having a lengthy chat. As a testament to Malcolm's charm, shortly afterwards the drug company agreed to provide the drugs at no cost to us. Finally it felt like things were starting to go our way.

We spent weeks in Toronto while Malcolm underwent the procedure followed by a lengthy recovery. While he spent his days in isolation, I visited when I was allowed. Entering his room required scrubbing my hands thoroughly and being covered from head to toe. When I wasn't at the hospital, I was either staying in a nearby hospice or bunking down at a friend's house. It was a grueling, painful process for Malcolm, but he made it through. When he was given the all-clear to leave the hospital, we left with high hopes. Surely this would do the trick—this is what he needed to turn the corner toward good health.

The cancer came back within a few months.

In 1997, the cancer spread to his left lung. It was confined to the lower lobe, so they thought they might be able to stop the spread to the rest of his lungs by removing it. Even now it's hard to look at the photos of Malcolm's back after the operation. The incision started above his shoulder blade, arced around the blade, and ended more than twelve inches further near his side. He called it his own, personal railway line.

Throughout all of the treatments, Malcolm was stoic and upbeat. Even after the bone-marrow transplant, Malcolm bounced back and, for a time, seemed perfectly normal. The lobectomy, however, was different. He never regained his usual strength after that. The pain in his back returned, and he developed a persistent shortness of breath. His weight began to dip downwards. His normally broad, strong shoulders and back muscles disappeared, leaving behind an emaciated body. He spent more and more time on the sofa with a heating pad on his back.

I never did go back to my PhD. The year of recovery on which I had pinned all my hopes had quickly evaporated. I now felt certain if I left, Malcolm would be unable to function alone, particularly in his business.

When I told my supervisor I had to withdraw, he was upset. He insisted I was throwing away a huge opportunity. Did I know how hard it was to get the scholarship I had won? Yes, I knew perfectly well. How could I throw out a bright future? I had come so far and was in such a good position to launch a strong academic career. How could I walk away from that? He suspected I would regret the decision. He understood I was in a difficult situation but felt strongly I shouldn't throw away all of my accomplishments.

My shoulders slumped as I thought about it. I knew he was right. I would deeply regret walking away from my PhD, but I could not imagine a single other option. How on earth could I leave my husband behind? What was I supposed to do—find a surrogate wife while I completed my studies?

That was the end of my PhD. I kept trying to tell myself I would go back as soon as I could and prove my supervisor wrong. I really believed it, but not for long. It soon became clear my academic career was decidedly over.

I couldn't dwell on it though; there was just too much work to be done. The more ill Malcolm became, the more the business flourished, and the more I became involved in the day-to-day operations. At first I helped with administrative work; then I took over planning. By the end, I was overseeing marketing, sales, planning, and production.

At the time of Malcolm's transplant, we were in the process of moving to a 3,000-square-foot production facility. We had hired a guy to do the bulk of the construction work inside the building, but the plan had also been to have Malcolm and his father do some of the work to save on costs. When Malcolm was unable to work, Ron handed me a drill, showed me how to install the floor, and then told me to get to work. He wasn't interested in my protests that I had never done that type of work before. Yes, I knew how to operate a drill, but there's a hell of a difference between assembling a piece of IKEA furniture and installing a wood floor in a 1,000-square-foot office. Ron was immovable. It had to be done, I had to get to work. My complaints were irrelevant.

When the flooring was done, I got a lesson in installing drywall. Between making sales calls and overseeing production of the stock, I would put up walls in our new offices alongside Ron. Whatever needed to be done, Ron handed me the appropriate tool, showed me how to use it, and set me to work.

In the spring of 1997, we bought a house and moved to a nearby hamlet just outside of Kingston. The house was a 1970s nightmare, but the location was lovely: 2.2 acres of land backing onto dense woods that sheltered deer, a couple of pileated woodpeckers, and thirty-one other species of birds. It became Malcolm's haven as he dealt with the worst of his illness. I hated the house, but I appreciated what it offered for Malcolm—a little bit of beauty in an otherwise ugly existence.

It was a stressful, awful time with no days off. I would drive Malcolm to his medical appointments, take him home afterwards, and then head back into the city to our production facility to work. I'd run back home to check on Malcolm, make him meals, and then head back to work. There was no respite from work or the constant strain of worrying about Malcolm's condition.

Despite the fact that Malcolm never complained about his pain, I could see he was getting worse. On occasion he would head over to his drafting table to draw something, but soon enough he'd be back on the sofa with the ever-present heating pad.

He did manage to hold up reasonably well for a brief visit from my parents, though. They had flown in to spend a few days with us after Christmas. As soon as they were gone, he went back to his resting spot. When my parents left in the first few days of 1998, Malcolm and I thought we would finally have some time to spend alone, resting and reconnecting after a difficult year. Since January was a slow period for our business, we often took a few weeks off to recharge our batteries after a frenetic Christmas retail season. That year we especially needed it, however, Mother Nature had other plans.

On January 4th our area experienced a series of storms the likes of which it had never seen. These storms were later called the Great Canadian Ice Storm. Everywhere we looked there was ice. Hydro wires had collapsed, roads were impassible, and most of the houses in our area had no power, including ours. Our outage lasted for five days.

Imagine it: it's the beginning of January, it's freezing cold, and there's no power. You can't leave the house because the entire landscape is a sheet of ice—you can't drive or walk anywhere. Since we lived out in the country, we also didn't have municipal water, which meant we relied on a pump powered by electricity to draw water from the well, so we also had no water.

All of this happened at a time when Malcolm couldn't do much physically. Thankfully we had some chopped wood in the garage and a wood-burning fireplace in the family room at the far end of the house, so he kept the fire going while I gathered snow to melt and then boil for water, which we then used to flush our toilets and to cook. I hauled out our camping gear, emptied the contents of the fridge into a cooler that sat on the deck, and for five days we lived in the family room in front of the wood stove. We ate whatever we could cook on the surface of the stove. Thank heavens we had food in the fridge!

The rest of that winter passed by in a blur, much like my twenties. Before I knew it, I had turned thirty-two, had bought a house in the country—something I swore I would never do—and I was on a hamster wheel that was turning faster and faster.

Until it stopped.

JOURNEY TO THE LAKE

Today, there is no joke.

— DAN, COLLEAGUE OF MALCOLM'S

I was away at a trade show when I received a panicked call from Ron. Malcolm had collapsed in the house, but he'd had the presence of mind to call 911. Firemen had kicked in our front door so the paramedics could get to him. He was rushed to the hospital, where doctors discovered that one of his lungs had hemorrhaged. By the time I got to him he was in stable but serious condition at the hospital.

I was in shock. There was another trade show coming up, which required a great deal of preparation, and my husband was in the hospital facing a very serious condition. I went into survival mode, which means you don't think, you do. I worked twelve-hour days, and in between I spent roughly six hours a day with Malcolm in the hospital.

During one of our visits, Malcolm told me about a dream he'd just had, in which he found himself in a clear blue lake. He was floating peacefully underwater and, for the first time in years, he did not feel pain. There was no feeling of drowning or panic; it was a beautiful, safe, welcoming place for him. He couldn't remember the last time he had woken up feeling so light and relaxed.

Then our conversation turned to more practical considerations: the next trade show taking place in a few days. I wanted to cancel it. Something inside told me I needed to stay with Malcolm, but he wouldn't hear of it. He insisted the trade show was critical for our business, and besides, he would be right here when I got back. No big deal.

The next day when I came to say goodbye on my way to the trade show, which was four hours away, I couldn't do it. I could not say the word "goodbye." I began to cry without really understanding why. Malcolm took my hand and reassured me all would be well.

"It's okay. You'll be back in a few days. I'll see you soon. I love you," he said.

That was the last time I spoke with him. Two days later I got another panicked call from his father. Malcolm was in the intensive care unit, unconscious and intubated. I needed to rush back right away.

I don't remember the drive home. I'm grateful to whoever kept me safe as I sped directly to the hospital. I was not prepared for what I saw. Despite everything I had seen over the years, I had never seen him looking like that. My heart shattered. I held his hand and gave him hell for breaking his promise to me. "We were supposed to talk again soon, remember?"

My sister, a doctor, flew out to be with me at the hospital. She asked to see the latest x-rays of his lungs. The doctors agreed, and we sat side by side to view them. As soon as she saw them, she began to cry. She explained to me what she saw. Something, likely cancer, had invaded the bulk of his lungs. It was over.

On August 10, 1998 I made the hardest decision of my life: Malcolm's doctors needed permission to unplug his machines. Our closest friends were summoned and given a chance to say good-bye; then Malcolm's family had some time alone with him. Finally, it was my turn.

As I held his hand, I was mute. How on earth could I put nearly ten years into words? How could I convey exactly what he meant to me? When it comes right down to a final moment, to the very last words you will ever speak to someone, what do you say? What would you say? Every possible word seems so inadequate and insufficient. There is simply no place to start or to end.

Eventually I spoke. I told him it was time to go to the lake, that he would be well there, and that I would eventually see him again but not for a while. I held his hand and stared in disbelief, refusing to say good-bye. I kissed his forehead and stroked his gorgeous hair for the last time.

Malcolm's family was called back in. I nodded to the medical staff, and the respirator was unplugged. Within seconds the heart monitor flat-lined. He was gone.

After everyone had left, I sat with him in the now-silent ICU room. He looked so peaceful. For a brief moment I thought I could wake him, just give him a gentle nudge, and he'd wake up. Then it hit me: he was really gone.

I can't describe the feeling of having to let go of his hand and walk away, leaving him behind, knowing I would never again see him. Knowing that when I'm gone, the staff will wheel him down to the morgue. Knowing that when I step out of the hospital doors, the world will look unchanged. Students would be strolling by, arms laden with books. People would be rushing to get home.

The world would continue to move forward as it always had, but my brain would shut down because it could not reconcile what I was seeing with the fact that my world had come to a dead stop.

The hurt didn't set in right away. It couldn't. I was in shock.

It was not possible that Malcolm was dead. Everywhere around me were signs of his life—his clothes, his artwork, his unfinished projects, and the books he was reading. Malcolm *is* my husband, not *was*. Yet Malcolm was not there. I couldn't believe there would be no more conversations, no more hikes through the woods, no more snuggling on the sofa in front of the fireplace, no more life with Malcolm.

Family and friends arrived from everywhere to offer support and to help with funeral preparations. I hid in Ron's house for part of that time, trying to figure out how to send Malcolm off in a way that would honor his tremendous creativity. I couldn't bring myself to go to the funeral home to discuss options, so Ron went alone. He came back looking bleak.

Nothing seemed to suit Malcolm. Then he remarked that he had seen a plain pine box hidden in the corner, and he joked that it looked like something Malcolm had built.

That was it. Malcolm would be placed in a pine box, and everyone would be given a marker with which to write their final message to him directly on the box. He had spent most of his adulthood drawing for others and making them smile. Now it was their turn to draw something for him. The result was incredible, hilarious, and deeply moving. Malcolm lay surrounded by evidence of the many lives he had touched—funny drawings, touching messages, reminiscences, poems, and bad jokes.

Two days before the funeral, Ron asked me if I had written my eulogy. I had not. Ron was a warm Scotsman, but he could also be stern. He was a well-liked high school English teacher whose eyebrows alone could quiet an entire classroom. All of his students knew Mr. Gilbertson demanded clear thinking and precise language.

He handed me some paper and a pen and told me to get to it. When he returned an hour or so later, he asked again.

"Yes, I've done it."

"May I read it?"

I handed it to him. He read it without expression and gave it back to me.

"You can do better than that."

For half a second, I gawked at him in disbelief. I thought to myself, "Seriously Ron, you're going to critique my eulogy for your son as if it were a grade twelve writing assignment?" Then it dawned on me that, damn it all, he was right. So I swallowed my pride and wrote a better eulogy.

Funerals are deeply cathartic for friends and family. There is much expression of love and sadness followed by a celebration of life. Once it's over though, everyone returns to their normal lives, and that's when the hurt really sets in. When you have to face the silence of your house and your life, you realize all too quickly how truly alone you are.

For the first time in my life, I felt deep and complete loss.

5

DOORS CLOSE

I've cried, and you'd think I'd be better for it,
but the sadness just sleeps, and it stays in
my spine the rest of my life.

— CONOR OBERST

My friends Andrea and Jeff stayed with me for the first week after the funeral. I was such an emotional mess I could not function. Jeff tackled Malcolm's computer and tried to sort out some of the graphic files for the upcoming Christmas sales season, while Andrea looked into bills and made phone calls. One of those calls was to Revenue Canada to explain that the Goods and Services Tax return would be late but filed as soon as I could get back on my feet. I don't know what I would have done without their help.

Once they left, I spent the next three weeks sitting on the floor of my house, crying. The phone rang, but I couldn't move. The only person I saw was Ron, who came by daily. He was as distraught as I was. Together we would alternate between silence, tears, and discussions of the senselessness of Malcolm's loss. There is something terribly wrong about a child dying before the parent, Ron would say.

I had virtually stopped eating. Those who know me know I love food. It had always mystified me how some people could forget to eat. No one had ever needed to remind me to eat three solid meals a day. Now they did. Ron pleaded with me to eat something, anything, so I drove to the grocery store, grabbed a cart, and walked through the aisles in a daze. Nothing made sense—cans, bags, boxes, produce—what was all this stuff? What did I need? I panicked and ran out empty-handed, abandoning the cart in the middle of the store.

One of the contributing factors in my mental deterioration was the disappearance of my normally rock-solid sleep patterns. Sleep was elusive despite my overwhelming feeling of exhaustion. I would sit in bed and stare at the empty space beside me. Malcolm's books were still on the bedside table, and his clothes were still hanging in our closet. It was inconceivable that he would not be back. When I wasn't stuck in a state of shock, I was haunted by memories of his last days in hospital. Why hadn't I stayed behind and cancelled the trade show? What on earth was I thinking? Why was I so stupid?

The fog and the incapacity continued for two months until one day, in a moment of clarity, panic set in. I realized for the first time that part of my future had died with Malcolm. Yes, I ran the business and yes, I helped to generate our products, but he was the engine that drove all else. Without his artwork and ideas, our business was dead. It was as though someone had just turned off the switch to my income. How would I pay off our debts? How would I survive financially?

I had a big money problem: big debts, no savings, and soon there would also be no income. Our business had generated excellent cash flow over the years, however, much of it had been spent dealing with Malcolm's illness. Since we were self-employed, we did not have health insurance beyond what was covered by our government. Those who think that all health care is free in Canada have clearly not dealt with a major illness. Every year we spent tens of thousands of dollars on Malcolm's medical care—medications, equipment, supporting therapies like massage and physiotherapy, parking at the hospital and medical clinics, and eating there when visiting—not to mention the cost of lost productivity. It was a case of one step forward, two steps back. Consequently, the cupboard was nearly bare when Malcolm died.

Sadly, there was no insurance to fall back on, either. Cancer patients who have the misfortune of having cancer their entire lives are uninsurable. There was, nonetheless, the funeral to pay for and hundreds of thousands of dollars' worth of business liabilities to be addressed over and above the mortgage for a house which we had just purchased the year before. When everything was added up, I had debts in the hundreds of thousands of dollars with a stalled income. Cue a full-blown panic.

There was no longer any time for grieving. I had to get to work to survive the looming Christmas season. Two thirds of our income was generated in that all-important season from October to December, with preparations typically beginning in July. I had done little that summer since Malcolm had spent most of July and the first ten days of August in the hospital. My life throughout that period revolved around dealing with his rapid decline and then his death. If I was going to survive the year, I needed to make money.

For the next sixty days, I worked fourteen hours a day, seven days a week, and traveled to six cities to ensure the usual Christmas sales. Thankfully Malcolm had already produced the designs for the year, and Jeff had stepped in to produce all of the graphic files required. The year before Malcolm's death we had subcontracted out all production, so I needed to hire staff only as required for preparations and shipments.

I made it through my first Christmas season without Malcolm. It was an awful, joyless time. Customers would come into our booth and laugh uproariously at some of the humorous items, often asking me who created the products.

"My husband and I did," I would answer.

"You must have the best marriage!"

I would complete the sales and escape as quickly as possible into the washroom to cry behind a stall door. After a while I would douse my face with cold water to minimize the swelling around my eyes, and return to the booth. The season mercifully came to an end.

I returned home to my empty house and locked myself in. Ron wanted me to join them at their house for a much-diminished Christmas dinner, but I refused. A friend called to see if she could visit; I declined. I did not want to be around anyone, and I certainly did not want to participate in anything festive. Screw the tree, the decorations, the gifts, and the turkey dinner. Peace, joy, and goodwill were for others who had not just lost their husband. I needed to grieve alone.

On Christmas day, I made a massive bowl of popcorn, brought out a bottle of Highland Park Scotch, and watched the BBC production of *Pride and Prejudice* from beginning to end, twice. I racked up roughly fourteen hours of television viewing. I remember nothing else from that Christmas break.

January brought with it a new gloom as I thought about my future. I could continue to run the business with our existing designs for one, perhaps two years at most, but without new material, sales would dwindle quickly. Added to that, I had never liked the work. This had been Malcolm's dream, not mine. I obviously had to reinvent myself and do so quickly.

Close friends had counseled me to follow my interests, but I no longer had any idea what my interests were. For the past six years I had focused entirely on my husband's health and our business. My life revolved around cancer and financial survival. Who knew what I liked or wanted anymore? Certainly not me.

Life was so stressful during that time I felt like my brain would explode from all the pressure. In order to blow off some steam I began taking pavement-pounding walks along my country road at night, having chats—or more like rants—with the universe and expressing deep anger about my situation. I needed some time away from this life, to reconnect with myself, to make up for the decade spent in oncology wards, and decide what I wanted to be when I grew out of the grief and pain I was drowning in.

In the absence of an ideal solution, I decided to complete the business year, sell all the remaining assets, including my house, and then spend one year traveling around Australia and New Zealand. Why Australia and New Zealand? No clue. They just seemed like the furthest point from my existing life, perfectly suited for running away. Plus, the weather is a lot more attractive than the stuff I faced in Kingston. Sun, sand, ocean waves, great wine, friendly people, and no reminders of what I had just been through. Yes, that was just what I needed.

Finally, I had a plan, and while I was still grieving Malcolm's loss, I began to see a means of escape. It was at that time I received a letter from the Canada Revenue Agency informing me that they wanted to audit my business.

There must be some mistake. I called them immediately and asked what this was about—yes, they wanted an audit. I was apparently selected randomly. Could this be because I had submitted a couple of returns very late following my husband's death? They had no answer for that. But my husband died, and I'm only just starting to catch up on the backlog of paperwork now. They would not budge. Are you kidding me? You want to audit me after everything I've been through? Have you experienced loss? Do you have any idea what this is like?

"When can we come over to begin the audit?"

When hell freezes over.

I eventually complied, figuring they could make my life even more of a living hell if I didn't. They came, looked through everything, and left, saying that they were satisfied. I was numb. Not cool Universe, not cool.

The next twelve months were spent preparing to shed every vestige of my business life. I organized the final Christmas season, planned the sale of the house, sold off assets, gave away all of Malcolm's art equipment to a local high school, and for the first time in fourteen months, I began to sort through Malcolm's personal items. It was time.

It was difficult to let go of his things, but there was one upside. Malcolm had owned a couple of pairs of really ugly briefs he'd refused to throw out despite my pleas.

"You realize I'm never going to touch you when you're wearing those, right?" I'd say.

He'd smile, be charming, and hold on to the uglies. I joked with him that if he ever died the first thing I would do was burn those underwear.

And that's precisely what I did when I got around to dealing with his clothes. When I opened the dresser drawer containing his briefs and found the two specimens I had loathed, I smiled. I promptly lit a fire in the wood stove and opened a nice bottle of wine. Then, with a toast and a reminder to Malcolm that I was simply following through on my promise, I tossed in the underwear and watched the cotton burn beautifully. Problem solved.

"You knew I'd get the last word in on this one, didn't you?"

When the last of the items was gone, I sat on the floor of Malcolm's now-empty art room, poured myself another glass of wine, and asked him for guidance.

"OK, now what?"

DOORS OPEN

Left alone, no matter at what age or under what
circumstance, you have to remake your life.

— Katharine Graham

I was lonely.

Malcolm had been gone for more than two years when I
finally decided to open myself up to the possibility of sharing
my life with another man. Everywhere I looked, I saw happy couples,
and it made me yearn for someone to talk to again, someone to laugh
with. *I* wanted to be the girl strolling down the street holding my guy's
hand, *I* wanted to have a date to the movies or to dinner, and *I* wanted
to be the girl who puts her freezing toes on her warm guy's legs at night.
As much as I missed Malcolm desperately, I understood he was gone
forever. If I wanted that lovely closeness in my life once again, I'd have
to allow it to happen.

But where do you find a great guy when you're 34? Well-intentioned
friends had tried to introduce me to single men with disastrous results.

Painful dinners ensued. The pity and awkwardness was mortifying and awful. I spent most dinners with a smile pasted on my face, praying for a heart attack.

I needed to figure this out, so I went for a walk to have a chat with the universe. I saw my situation pretty clearly that night; I needed to write down what I was looking for. How could I expect to find what I wanted if I didn't have clarity to begin with? So, on September 22, 2000, I listed the top ten attributes I sought in a new life partner. Since I had the opportunity to start over, I would be very selective. I set the list aside and got down to work on the business's final Christmas season.

Two months later, Mark came into my life, or rather, he re-entered my life. Fourteen months before, I had hosted a memorial planting day at my house on the first anniversary of Malcolm's death. All family and friends were welcome to drop by to plant something in Malcolm's memory. They could plant anything they wanted and also select the location; there were no rules—just like Malcolm. We would then share a glass of wine, swap funny Malcolm stories, and celebrate his life.

It was a brilliantly sunny day. One friend, whose last name is McIntosh, brought a McIntosh apple tree, another brought a Dogwood, and others brought flowering shrubs or beautiful flowers. Then Mark arrived with his offering.

This is the point in the story where our children convulse with laughter. When I first shared this story with them, our oldest daughter turned to Mark and said, "Papa, what were you thinking?" to which Mark replied, "My lawyer has advised me not to answer that question."

Mark's parents are avid horticulturalists, each having been president of their local horticultural society many times over. Their lovely English garden consumes much of their time during the summer. Mark's mother even worked for a few years as the local expert in the gardening section of a large store. Given this, you might expect Mark to turn to his parents for advice and possibly even a sampling from their garden for the memorial planting. He did not. Instead, for reasons which are still a mystery to everyone, he plucked a single sunflower from a friend's garden on one of the hottest days of the year. When he emerged from his car, he was clutching a wilted, clinging-to-life sunflower. I have no idea where he planted it (it didn't survive long enough to be found); all I know is that I gave him a wry smile when I saw the thing. As a metaphor for Malcolm's life, it left a lot to be desired.

The guy redeemed himself moments later when he approached me with a bottle of Spanish Rioja he meant for us to share. From his description, it sounded like it would knock my socks off. It did. It really was that good. The guy had great taste in wine, so I forgave him for showing up with a dying flower that didn't survive the night.

As we sipped the wine we got to talking about other beverages we enjoy. I think he was surprised when he discovered I love single-malt Scotch and even more surprised at my collection of the stuff. As we compared favorites he mentioned he had one I really wanted to try. Soon he was inviting me over some time for a drink.

It all sounded very innocent to me, and frankly, that's how I took it. Malcolm had been gone only one year, and I was still deeply grieving his loss. When Mark made the offer, I viewed it strictly as an opportunity to try a Scotch that appealed to me. We set a date for the tasting.

The evening did not go well. To this day Mark and I disagree on the reason behind the failed evening, but the bottom line is that I tried the Scotch and loved it, but I walked away from the night thinking, "Well that was uncomfortable."

Naturally Ron lost no time in snooping for details.

"How did your date go?"

"It wasn't a date. I just went over to try the Balvenie, which is lovely by the way."

"Of course it was a date. If a man asks you over to his place for a drink, it's a date."

"That's an archaic view. It *is* possible to just share a love of Scotch and nothing more for an evening."

"Mmmm, yes."

"Besides, I wouldn't date him if he were the last man on earth. We're far too different."

Ron howled. "I see, he's Elmo then?"

"What?"

"L.M.O.E. Last Man On Earth?"

"Cut it out."

That was it, though. Mark would forever be known to Ron as LMOE.

Shortly after that, Mark left to travel throughout Australia and New Zealand for a year. While he was away he sent me a couple of post cards though I really wasn't sure why. We weren't exactly friends. Malcolm and Mark had gone to high school together, and later Mark had been a client of our business, but beyond that and our moments of shared wine and Scotch, we hardly knew each other.

When Mark returned from his travels, he reached out to a number of friends to reconnect. As part of that effort he sent me an email about a joke that was going on in Canadian politics at the time that involved my first name. When I asked him where he was, expecting to hear he was somewhere in Australia, he wrote back to say he was in Kingston. He then asked if I'd like to join him for "dinner/drinks/coffee/dancing/all of the above?"

I immediately wrote back declining the invitation. He and I were such different people. I did not want to get stuck in another awkward evening. I would never date the guy anyway, so why bother? Just as I was about to hit the "Send" button, something made me stop. I pulled back my chair, stared at the screen for a few seconds, rolled back up, erased everything I had previously written, and wrote something like this: "I'm only in town for forty-eight hours. If it's tonight or tomorrow night, then fine. Otherwise I'll see you in the spring." Then I hit "Send."

Less than five minutes later I got the following reply, "We have dinner reservations at *Le P'tit Chien Noir* for 7:00 tonight. I'll see you there." There was no backing out now.

On the drive to the restaurant I kept talking to myself. It's only dinner. Even if it's awful, it won't last long. He's a smart guy; you'll find something to talk about. Relax, it's only dinner, and you do need to eat. You can do this. What the hell were you thinking? You should have said no. You're an idiot! Maybe you can fake a fever.

I knew one thing about Mark: he had great taste in wine. If nothing else went well, I'd at least have some kick-ass wine to enjoy.

I took a deep breath and walked into the restaurant. Mark was already seated and had selected an excellent bottle of wine. To my surprise, the dinner went well. He admitted to me afterwards that during dinner he was going through his mental checklist of things he was looking for in a woman and checking them off. I did not confess that my thoughts had leaned more toward this possibly becoming a fling. My intention was to date casually and briefly. He had other plans.

A few days later I was in Toronto for a business show, thinking the fling had ended. I was staying at a friend's house, and one night she picked up the ringing phone and handed it to me.

"It's for you."

It was Mark, offering to come to Toronto to help with the show. I protested, telling him he was crazy, but he showed up anyway wearing a business suit and a killer "let me sell you something" smile. For him, an IT guy, this whole sales business was a lark, nothing but good times. I let him stay, figuring I could use the break. And, if he was dismal at it, I could yank him out of there.

As I watched from the sidelines, Mark sold up a storm, probably because he was having a great time. There was no pressure or down-side for him. He had bought the products in the past and enjoyed them, a fact which he shared with anyone who came near. The cash register dinged away as he rang up sales.

For me, the whole thing felt insane. I was in a different city on business with a guy I hardly knew who, incidentally, was selling my stuff. What the hell was I doing? Come to think of it, what the hell was he doing?

"Who's the cute guy with the great eyes?" overly curious fellow exhibitors would ask.

"Just a friend," I'd reply.

"Well, you be sure to be good to that *friend*. If you don't want him, send him my way!" said one. It was a long, long show filled with sly winks and knowing smiles.

Every night some of the exhibitors would meet at a nearby restaurant for a late dinner. The first night Mark was there we ended up off to the side, heads bent in discussion. We talked about all manner of things and then out of left field he asked me the weirdest thing.

"How do you feel about children?"

"What?"

"How do you feel about children? Do you want them?"

"You're kidding right? I'm not even sure that we're dating, and you're asking me about children?"

The funny thing is, he wasn't even sure where the question had come from either. Still, he was certain he wanted an answer. How on earth did I find these men?

"Honestly, I don't know how I feel about children. I don't think I want any. Malcolm couldn't have any and, since we were busy dealing with cancer treatments, I never really thought about it. Now I think I'd rather not have them. My friends who are parents don't seem to be having a great time. Their lives revolve around the kids, meals are eaten cold, there's less travel, less fun, more stress, less sex. That doesn't sound very appealing to me."

"That's a deal breaker for me. I want two kids."

"Wait a minute. A second ago you told me you hadn't really thought about kids until tonight, and now it's a deal-breaker for you? How does that add up?"

Mark shrugged. I was confused. Suddenly he had connected with a part of himself that really, really wanted children? Well tough crap. He was going to have to sit with that for a bit because I wasn't prepared to make a commitment either way. I had just spent twelve years going through emotional hell, and now that I was starting to see a light at the end of the tunnel, I wasn't prepared to entertain something as serious as children. I just wanted to have fun.

I didn't give him a definitive answer. Instead, I told him I would think about it, which was the best that I could do under the circumstances. If he wanted to be with me, he'd have to accept that. And he did. It was another display of two key traits that I have come to associate with Mark: patience and persistence.

Three weeks later, he made another trip out to left field. The question this time wasn't about children. This time, he proposed. It wasn't even a planned event with ring in hand; it just came blurting out in mid-sentence one evening.

It's ironic how we occasionally beg the universe for a solution to one of our desperate needs and when the universe delivers, we resist. "Yes but not *that* solution!" I had asked for a man; I had made a list and had been very specific. The universe dutifully sent me a man, and I panicked.

Another pavement-pounding walk and conversation with the universe ensued, in which I played both prosecutor and defense attorney.

"I can't do it. This is madness."

Why not? You're ready and so is he. This is what you've asked for.

"No, it's not what I asked for, and besides, he's not at all like Malcolm."

That's the idea. You *asked* for someone different. You made your list. Mark is great and you know it.

"Yes he is, but I'm not ready for this. Plus we are *so* different. It can't possibly work."

You're just afraid. That's understandable, but it's not an excuse.

"It's only been three weeks! Who the hell gets engaged after only three weeks?"

So what? Malcolm proposed after three days. By that measure Mark has taken his sweet time. And you have been waiting for two years to meet Mark.

"I've been a bit busy in that time. I haven't exactly spent those two years looking for a mate. It's too soon."

Stop trying to be the general manager of the universe, and let things unfold as they will.

"What about Australia and New Zealand?"

Good news. They're not going anywhere. They will still be around when you're ready to visit with Mark.

"Yes but. . . ."

The tug-of-war between head and heart continued for four months. Through it all, Mark was patient, understanding, and persistent. Eventually my fears receded and I accepted. We were married the following summer.

Sometime during that period of uncertainty I realized I had no clue about Mark's birthday, so I asked him about it. He hesitated. Good heavens, this wasn't a skill-testing question. What was with the hesitation?

"My birthday is August 10th."

I stared at him. Surely he wouldn't joke with me about *that*. He pulled out his driver's license to prove it. Sure enough, his birthday was August 10th. Every year now, on August 10th, I pay tribute to Malcolm, and I celebrate Mark's birthday.

Doors close and doors open.

PART II

Lessons

I n the chapters that follow, I summarize some of the key lessons I have learned since Malcolm's death. Many of them are related to my experience of becoming a widow and facing a financial crisis, but a few are whoppers learned long after I rebuilt my life, particularly the lesson regarding real estate investing.

If only we had the chance to turn back the clock! If someone had asked me, "If you had to do it over again, would you do anything differently?" my answer would be, "Hell, yes!" I would do a lot of things differently and save myself a lot of grief in the process. But, life being what it is, I did many things the hard way and offer the following lessons instead.

Interspersed in my lessons you will find other women's stories. It's great to read one woman's story, but I also wanted to explore the experience of others. I wanted to discover if what I went through was unique, or rather part of a larger, more universal experience of loss.

I'm not suggesting that anyone who experiences loss, whether through death or divorce, goes through exactly the same steps or emotions as the next person, but I did wonder if there is some common ground.

I have broken the other women's stories down into categories, mostly for reasons of presentation, though, as you'll soon read, several of the categories overlap.

One thing becomes clear as you hear from the women below: there are many common points among our individual experiences. While the details of each story vary, some of the underlying difficulties appear to be universal.

When the women had finished telling me their stories, I asked them two questions:

1. If you had known what was coming, what would you have done differently?

2. Given what you've been through, what advice do you have for women?

Their answers will no doubt surprise and inspire you.

WHAT TO SAY WHEN SOMEONE DIES

Sometimes the right thing gets done for the
wrong reason and sometimes, unfortunately,
the wrong thing gets done for the right reason.

— JAMES CARVILLE

It struck me after Malcolm's death just how bad we are, on the
whole, at dealing with death. You'd think since death is such an
integral part of being human, we would be pretty good by now
at knowing how to talk about it and how to reach out to the bereaved.

We're not. In fact, we don't typically talk about death because it
makes us feel uncomfortable. As a result, we struggle with knowing
what to say or do when someone experiences a tragic loss.

I can tell you the first few days after the death of a spouse are unreal.
The initial state of profound shock is followed by a deep, visceral pain of
loss. The surrounding signs of the spouse's life—his clothes, his phone
that still holds the last text message sent, his notes around the house, his
coffee cup on the counter—make it seem unfathomable that he is gone. It

is impossible to ever speak with him again. The children will never again see their father. Your brain shuts down, unable to cope with the contradiction of today's knowledge of his death with the ever-present evidence of his life. The grief is overwhelming, and nothing makes any sense.

Then there is the guilt and doubt. If he died suddenly, you relive every moment asking yourself what you could have done differently. You question every decision, every action, and every inaction. You beat yourself up and doubt yourself in ways that tear you apart even further. It is a soul-crushing time.

The first week or two you are surrounded by friends and family. The busy rush of telling the world and making sudden decisions about the funeral carry you through the haze of the first week after his death. There is so much to do and everyone wants to pitch in, but you have no idea what you need or how they can help. You can think only of getting the kids to school and planning the funeral—beyond that it's all an incomprehensible blur. You stop eating and sleeping, running on sheer adrenaline and stress.

So as a friend or family member, what can you do? Where do you start? What should you avoid? Here are a few ideas.

KEEP IT SIMPLE AND GENUINE

First and foremost, be genuine, speak from the heart, and keep it simple. A few years ago my friend Shawn died suddenly at the age of 39. As I read people's reactions on Facebook, I was deeply touched by their expressions of shock, compassion, condolence, sympathy, and of keeping his wife and their children in their thoughts and prayers. It was beautiful and perfect.

By reaching out initially you let the widow know that you have heard the news and are touched by her loss in a meaningful way. You're also letting her know she's not alone in her grief and that her husband touched the lives of many people. I cannot emphasize how important that is.

I would also encourage you to send a card even if you've called or emailed or replied on social media. The effort to send something hand-written is always appreciated and shows an additional level of care. I kept all of the cards I received when Malcolm died. I read them over and over again in the weeks following his death. It gave me a great deal of comfort to see how many people were mourning his loss, too and to hear about how he had touched their lives.

FOOD FIRST, FLOWERS LATER

The common practice following a death seems to be to send flowers. I suggest foregoing flowers initially and consider giving food instead. The last thing a widow wants to think about following the trauma of her husband's death is food. For the first week or so, she will be surrounded by family and friends who will likely cook for her and the children. But once everyone leaves, and they always do at some point, she will have to face all of the tasks by herself. Consider filling her freezer with meals she can cook or reheat at a moment's notice. Or, if you prefer, drop by two or three weeks after the funeral with a complete dinner in hand.

Here's the thing about flowers under these circumstances: they reek of death. A room full of flowers makes one think of a wedding or funeral. I had a house full of flowers after Malcolm died and, while I deeply appreciated the thought behind those expressions of sympathy, they also depressed me even more. They were constant reminders of death. Then, just as everyone else was getting back to their normal lives, I was left with a heap of wilting, dying flowers. More unfortunate symbolism.

Don't get me wrong, flowers are beautiful, and sending them represents an act of caring. But how about sending them to the widow three to five months later with a note that says something like "We're thinking of you and hope that these brighten your day." She's going to need a lot of brightening in six months' time when everyone around her has moved on and she's still left to pick up the pieces. It would be an unexpected blessing and a splash of color at a time when she needs it most.

TRUST FUND OR DONATION

It can be helpful to ask if the widow is financially solid. I realize this is a delicate topic, but one of the main reasons this book exists is because most women are not prepared for the death of their spouse. Far too many are left in a financially difficult position when their spouse's income disappears and there is insufficient insurance to ensure financial stability. It's also not cheap to die. Just ask anyone who has had to pay for a casket and a funeral.

If the widow is in good shape financially, you might consider making a donation to a charity that is meaningful to the deceased's family. If you don't know what would be appropriate, ask. They'll be touched by the gesture.

If she is facing financial hardship, consider starting a trust fund for her. My friends Andrea and Jeff did that for me when Malcolm died, and it made a significant difference in my life. They contacted the local newspaper, which ran a story about my situation and loss, and I found myself receiving donations from complete strangers. It was deeply touching and helpful at a time when I faced a myriad of difficulties.

SHARE YOUR MEMORIES

As I mentioned earlier, a widow is often well supported for the first week or two following the death, but after that, support wanes. This is not a judgment, it's just a reflection of the reality that everyone gets pulled back into their lives and daily routines fairly quickly. While that's understandable, the fact remains that the widow's grief will not end a week or two after the funeral. In fact, it will intensify. This is when she will need your support the most.

One of the simplest ways to support her is to share your favorite stories and photos of her husband. One month after the death, send her a note sharing a favorite memory. A few months later perhaps send a photo of him that made you laugh or smile. Tell a story, your story of an event with the deceased.

For months after Malcolm died, I received cards and letters from people all over the world who wanted to share their memories of Malcolm. It was their way of honoring his memory and paying tribute to him while connecting with me. Many of these people were complete strangers— I had never even heard of them. And yet, here they were telling me about touching stories and hilarious escapades with Malcolm, the kind of stuff that would have had everyone's eyes watering if told at a party.

These stories made me laugh and made me cry too, but mostly I was delighted to discover these fun, moving stories about how Malcolm had touched their lives. They were so important to me, I created an album of all the correspondence.

Here are a few examples of the notes I received, one from the guy who became my husband a few years later:

"I just heard about Malcolm's death and am totally without words to express how I feel. My sympathies and thoughts are with you. For me, as a customer, I only knew Malcolm from his work. I get the feeling he did what he did because he enjoyed it. Not everyone can say that. I feel honored to have part of his legacy, his humor."

". . . I suppose the one thing that actually does stand out from the long drive we once took together is that we asked each other "If there was something you'd change in your life, what would it be?" I foolishly expected Malcolm to say the obvious—a cancer-free life—but that's not what he said. He wanted to give you, Doris, an extended period of hospital-free, medical-worry-free days. And he wanted desperately to take you on a long holiday. I know my brain went "HOLY F**K DORIS! You are an extraordinarily lucky woman."

— A MUTUAL FRIEND

". . . A few things to which I can testify: Malcolm had a jugular wit. He liked the northern woods. He liked to cut them down. He preferred the chainsaw and I preferred the ax. We had many long, philosophical discussions on the relative merits of both, which usually ended with us "agreeing to disagree." That, or a duel of Schnapps shots."

— A FRIEND OF MALCOLM'S

"I have a particularly lovely memory of Malcolm, and since you were a part of it (although you didn't know it at the time), I would like you to have it too. It was the last night he was in the ICU in July. He was feeling a bit stronger, although he was still very weak. I had seen him several times a day, although I had missed you, unfortunately, and we had had brief visits.

This evening though, it was quiet; he was waiting for you to come, and we visited over half an hour. We talked about his enthusiasm for the contract you were involved in negotiating; his favorite shirts (my son wears them all the time), his hopes and plans for the future, how much he loved your home in the country, the options for his treatments, your recent trip with your family in the mountains, and how important you were to him. I had to leave before you came, and I asked him to say hello to you, that you were a very special woman. He smiled lopsidedly, nodded his head, and with rare seriousness agreed, "She certainly is." We were both quiet for a few moments. Then he smiled again and waved goodnight.

As it turned out, that was the last time we spoke. I am so grateful to have had that conversation. It so characteristically reflected not his illness but the richness of his life, his interests, and his love for you. I wish you had been there.

I cannot presume to know what it is like for you now. I simply wanted you to know that Malcolm was a special person to me, and you two were a remarkable couple. I will miss him and remember you both. It was a real privilege to help care for him."

— ONE OF HIS DOCTORS

"Doris, I promised a few more memories of Malcolm . . . When L and I came out to your house for Christmas last year, I spoke to Ron for a while about his retirement. I recall Malcolm making a special effort to sit down and make me feel welcome. We talked for a bit. Among many other things, we discussed the qualities of various Scotch whiskies, Tim Burton, and just about everything else. As everyone started to open presents, Malcolm realized I didn't have one. In spite of my protests he rushed around and found a jar of Rootham's Saskatoon berry jam. Since we Jews don't normally exchange Christmas presents, Malcolm gave me one of my first. Your friend, Mark. PS If you would like to go out for dinner, glass of wine, coffee . . . give me a call."

— MY FUTURE HUSBAND

The excerpts I shared above are just a sample of many kinds of stories and comments I received. I reread every note dozens of times in the months after Malcolm's death. They were a tremendous comfort to me during the hardest days. I learned you don't need to be a poet—just share your memories and thoughts from the heart. I can assure you that they will be appreciated.

One of the things I noticed after Malcolm died is that some people avoided talking to me about him. I suspect they did so to avoid upsetting me, but here's the thing: we want to talk about the people we've lost; we *need* to talk about them. Don't be afraid to keep mentioning the deceased's name. If something reminds you of him, say so, even if it makes the widow cry. Crying is a necessary part of grieving and healing, so instead of apologizing for making her cry, perhaps empathize with her.

I distinctly remember a conversation in which a good friend mentioned Malcolm's name many months after his death, and it set me off. Instead of looking uncomfortable, he gave me a hug and said, "I know, I miss him too." I was so grateful to him for that beautiful moment. He allowed me to express my grief without embarrassment, while at the same time letting me know that he, too, was feeling Malcolm's loss.

IT'S ALL IN THE QUESTION

Roughly one week after Malcolm died, I got a call from the funeral director that Malcolm's ashes were ready to be picked up. When I showed up, he handed me the urn and stared at me, clearly uncomfortable. This from a funeral director. You know, if anyone is going to be comfortable dealing with death, you'd think it would be a funeral director. Perhaps he was more accustomed to dealing with a more elderly clientele. In any case, as I turned to leave he said, "Are you okay?" I wish I could say that I said something gracious, but I didn't. Instead I replied, "I'm taking my husband home in an urn. No, I'm not okay."

I know he meant well, but I was so raw with grief I could not find it in me to reply with a customary, trite phrase.

Here's a suggestion about what not to ask a widow; don't ask her how she's doing. The majority of the time you can bet she's doing terribly. If she says otherwise, it's probably a polite lie to make you less uncomfortable. Instead consider asking, "How are you today?" Make it about today. Today is the only day that really matters for her because, in the beginning, it's far too painful to think about tomorrow. If she's having a hard time that day, ask how you can help make her day better. Baby steps. One day at a time. Help her focus on making today a bit better, then the next day a bit better, and so on.

Keep checking in with her, too. Set it as a reminder in your electronic calendar to reach out, so that you don't forget, because you can bet she won't forget about the loss.

Here are a few other ideas sent to me by readers of my blog when I first posted the ideas discussed above:

"I wanted to share something a small group of us did when one of our dear friends dropped dead and left behind his wife, who was a stay-at-home mom, and two young daughters.

I started a quiet campaign amongst a group of friends to gather money. The widow is a very private person and we all felt that if we'd set up a trust fund, it would be too public for her. We then nominated the most gentle of our friends to present her with a check because we were worried it would be a hard gift for her to accept. The card that went with the check said something to the effect of 'We want to help and hope this gift isn't too hard to accept. Please use this money in a way that helps, and know that none of us will ask or speak about it again.' For this particular friend we tried very hard to make it easy for her to accept it with dignity."

"When our first was born, about a month premature, we spent nearly a month of twenty-hour days at the hospital, praying we'd get through one week without an apnea spell so we could all go home. One gift we received that we will never forget, was a cooler filled with a pork tenderloin, potatoes and vegetables, plates, glassware, cutlery, and simple instruction: Reheat . . . Eat . . . Place dirty dishes back in cooler and return to us whenever you have the time."

I received the following advice from Charlynne MacCharles, a grief counselor:

"As you mentioned, Doris, at first when you are grieving, there are a lot of people offering support. It means so much when someone reaches out to you months later to let you know they are thinking of you. Making a phone call or sending a card on days that are especially difficult—the loved one's birthday, Valentine's Day, wedding anniversary, and other special occasions.

As friends, it's important to remember to reach out even when you don't get a response. It brings comfort to the person grieving to get messages and to know others are thinking of them. We want to avoid saying "How are you?" or "I hope you are doing okay," even months after the loss because the person might feel pressure to say "Yes, I'm fine." Some of my clients have said it doesn't give them the space to be open and honest about their grief.

Helping with practical matters tends to be deeply appreciated. Try to be specific when offering to help: "I'm going to the store—do you need bread, milk, or other groceries? I'll get them and drop them off for you." It's not as helpful to say "Call me if there is anything I can do," because when people are grieving they are already dealing with so many emotions and tasks that they won't necessarily reach out. Many of my grieving clients are afraid of imposing on their friends and family and worry that they will burden them if they ask for help."

The pain does eventually give way to a kind of acceptance, but it is a long, hard process. There is no getting over a significant loss. Even when the trauma turns to healing, there will always be a deep scar. Be patient with the widow, and know that hers is a path that will be her own, one which you cannot understand. The best you can do is offer support, patience, and acceptance as she makes her way through it.

GETTING STUCK IN THE TREES

I find greater value in what specific individuals
tell me worked for them than in any other kind
of argument—and that's true even when we
seem to have nothing in common.

— GRETCHEN RUBIN

I have learned that when you're in a crisis, the last thing you
have time for is reflection. Stress, fatigue, deadlines, difficult
decisions—these aren't exactly optimal conditions for deep
thoughts about the best path for your life. Just think about the last time
you went through a "holy crap" situation; you know, the kind that sets
off every panic button in your body. Did you take the time to think
things through properly, or did you just react as best you could under
the circumstances? Most of us do the latter.

The problem with this kind of fire-fighting approach is that it rarely
leads to the best decisions, and sometimes there may even be disastrous,
unintended consequences. The approach may meet an urgent, need but

it might not serve you in the long run. Now compound that with daily decisions to meet immediate needs. Where do you end up?

The thing about life is that it's insanely busy, and what's worse is that it just seems to be getting busier as the weeks go by. Between your work deadlines, your spouse's schedule, homework, the kids' activities, house maintenance, get-togethers with your friends, occasional trips to the gym and the interminable to-do list that nags you daily, there just aren't enough hours in a day to think. So you keep forging along with your gaze stuck squarely on the million-and-one daily details that need your attention until one day, you lift up your head and you realize that ten years have gone by. You're also nowhere near the destination you had in mind originally.

What on earth happened? Where did the time go? When you were twenty, you might have thought, "That won't happen to me." And then it did.

Life happens to us all. And life usually has us forging along in and out of the trees, trying to get to the next tree

IF YOU RETAIN ONLY ONE THING FROM THIS BOOK, I HOPE IT'S THIS POINT: BUILD THINKING TIME INTO YOUR LIFE AT REGULAR INTERVALS, AND THEN DURING THOSE MOMENTS OF REFLECTION, ASK A FEW IMPORTANT QUESTIONS:

- WHAT DO I REALLY WANT?
- AM I ON TRACK?
- WHAT IF MY SPOUSE GETS SICK OR DIES OR DISAPPEARS DOWN SOUTH WITH THE LOCAL BARISTA? WHAT THEN?
- WHAT IF I GET SICK?
- WHAT IF ONE OF MY KIDS GETS SICK?
- AM I IN CONTROL OF MY INCOME? IF NOT, WHAT CONTROLS IT, AND WHAT IS MY PLAN IN THE EVENT THAT THE SOURCE OF MY INCOME IS WITHDRAWN (E.G., LOSS OF JOB, BUSINESS FAILURE, DIVORCE)?
- AM I DOING WHAT I LOVE AND MAKING THE BEST USE OF MY GIFTS AND TALENTS? IF NOT, WHAT IS MY PLAN TO DO SO AS QUICKLY AS POSSIBLE?

and then the next. The problem is, if you never step back to look at the forest, you have no idea if you're headed in the right direction. Are you even in the right forest?

When I started down the path of becoming an academic, I had my whole future mapped out. I knew exactly where I was going and I was on track right up until Malcolm got sick. Then I went into panic-reactionary mode. I would make one local decision to deal with the first emergency, and then another, until I found myself in a big mess at the age of 32 wondering what the hell had happened to me.

If you retain only one thing from this book, I hope it's this point: Build thinking time into your life at regular intervals, and then, during those moments of reflection, ask a few important questions:

◈ What do I really want?

◈ Am I on track?

◈ What if my spouse gets sick or dies or disappears down south with the local barista? What then?

◈ What if I get sick?

◈ What if one of my kids gets sick?

◈ Am I in control of my income? If not, what controls it, and what is my plan in the event that the source of my income is withdrawn (e.g., loss of job, business failure, divorce)?

◈ Am I doing what I love and making the best use of my gifts and talents? If not, what is my plan to do so as quickly as possible?

Are you asking the right questions so that your life consists of a series of conscious choices rather than unconscious consequences? Remember the well-known maxim: If you fail to plan, you plan to fail.

Take some time to think about where you want to go with your one and only life, then chart the course. Keep checking in at regular intervals to ensure that you're headed in the right direction. This step alone can transform your results.

Hold on, you might say. Imagining a heap of nasty scenarios is a completely pessimistic way to approach life, and surely that's not what you're after. No, it's not. This is about planning.

I am an optimistic person. I can remember feeling furious when one of Malcolm's oncologists pretty much told me that Malcolm would probably die before his thirtieth birthday. (This is the same guy who told Malcolm that he would be lucky to see eighteen.) At the time I felt that he was robbing us of hope. Who was he to be playing God anyway? Sure, the odds were not in Malcolm's favor, but the chances of surviving were not zero, so why not focus on the positive and aim for that?

This kind of approach has served me well. It has meant I have kept going through dark times because I kept my eyes firmly fixed on the prize. And to this day, I recommend that people focus squarely on the goals they want to achieve, not on the road blocks in their way. There's a sure way to hit a road block: just keep looking at it. If you want to make it past inevitable challenges, you need to keep your goals front and center.

That said, this same approach has also done me considerable harm. In my twenties and early thirties, I was so determined to focus on the positive outcome that I failed to consider the alternatives. If, every step of the way, I had asked the simple question, "What if?" my experience would doubtless have been transformed, and I would not have written this book. I'm not saying that Malcolm would have lived, but I am saying that I would not have been left with massive debts, having to rebuild my life from scratch in my early thirties, a process which took nearly ten years.

I knew from the beginning that Malcolm had cancer, and as you've read, it became active early on in our life together. I was still completing my undergraduate degree when Malcolm had surgery to remove a cancerous node, followed by radiation treatments. At that time, I should have asked myself: What will happen if this gets worse? What impact will this have on my personal and academic life? What will I do if he becomes so ill that he is unable to work?

It is neither easy nor fun to ask "What if?" You probably won't like the answers. I know I wouldn't have in the early days had I asked that simple question. It can get complicated, painful, and messy to consider an unpleasant outcome, however, avoiding it won't alter the odds of it transpiring. If the worst does happen, the consequences are all too real.

But what do you do if the answer *is* complicated? Take my situation, for instance. I loved Malcolm and I wasn't going to walk away because he had cancer. What do you do then?

With the advantage of nearly twenty years of experience under my belt, I can now answer that question: you do the best you can, but you do not sacrifice your well-being and your future. Making yourself vulnerable and weak for the sake of helping someone else serves no one. I say this knowing what's on the line for a lot of women who have very hard choices to make.

In my case, my physical health was not at risk, but my financial health certainly was. When I walked away from my PhD, I set myself up for a world of trouble. A moment of deep reflection would have uncovered a few basic facts.

MAKING YOURSELF VULNERABLE AND WEAK FOR THE SAKE OF HELPING SOMEONE ELSE SERVES NO ONE.

First, Malcolm's business was in start-up mode and had no established sales. A lot of work was required to generate sales. Since I had no business training of any kind, I was not qualified to guide the business through its infancy. It would mean a lot of work and a massive learning curve.

Is that really what I wanted to do? Would I enjoy the work? Was the business viable? Would it pay me what I wanted and deserved to be paid? What future did it offer me?

Second, the sales were entirely dependent on Malcolm. He was the source of the designs on which the business was built. No Malcolm, no sales, at least not for long. I tried to find an artist who could take over the line after Malcolm's death, but that proved to be impossible. Others could copy existing material, but they could not duplicate the wit and apply it to new, original designs. Every attempt fell well below the mark.

Third, it was difficult to establish a source of recurring revenue given the nature of the products. While we could rely on some of our top-selling designs to bring in a lot of revenue, we knew that we had to keep replenishing the source of the designs. Therefore every design had a shelf life.

Here's a different example to illustrate the difficulty: There's a coffee shop in our city that Mark loves. He keeps going back to replenish his supply of beans every couple of weeks, sometimes more frequently. He will continue to do that forever along with hundreds of other people because they love the product, and it's a consumable. Eventually, their supply runs out. With a t-shirt design, once you have the shirt, you don't need a duplicate. You might think it's terrific enough to buy for a friend as a gift, but beyond that, you're not going to keep buying it. You might also buy it on another product like a greeting card, but there's a finite number of times you will buy the same design. If we want to keep you as a customer, we have to come up with other designs first, and then other products that will entice you to buy. Once the supply of designs runs out, so does the runway for the business. We can extend it a bit by finding new markets but really, the business's days are numbered without new designs.

By tying myself to Malcolm's business, I made myself entirely dependent on him as he was necessary to the business' survival. If something happened to him, the business would be in jeopardy. The man had cancer, and while it is certainly not a death sentence for most people, Malcolm's history did suggest that death was a very real possibility.

I also burned the bridge to the obvious plan B: returning to my studies. With every passing year, my work became more and more dated. If I wanted to get back to my PhD, I would have to start from scratch with no funding. Sure I could apply for the same scholarship but after having abandoned it several years back with no academic work under my belt in the interim, my chances weren't great. The only way to survive financially through another round of studies was to get a student loan or to work at a part-time job. Either way it would mean burning the candle at both ends and being broke all the time. Not appealing in the slightest.

None of this entered into my thinking when I walked away from my PhD because I was too busy doing everything I could to help Malcolm. Cancer had changed my world, and it was all I focused on. The irony of my situation is obvious now: the academic, whose job it was to spend her days thinking and researching, did not take the time to think about her own difficult situation in order to make a sound, reasoned choice. In other words, I did not think—I just acted.

I have asked myself a thousand times why on earth I didn't do what I was trained to do, which is to step back and look at the situation with clear eyes. It's only in the last five years or so that I've been able to admit to myself it was because I was afraid. It's painful to consider your spouse's death, particularly when it's a real possibility, so I avoided it. I was also determined to focus on a positive outcome, as though even thinking about his death might somehow increase the odds of it coming to pass. It's absurd, of course. Thinking about what you would do if something bad were to happen doesn't make the negative event any more likely to happen. I'm not talking about dwelling on a negative outcome here, just considering it as a possibility and figuring out what you would do in that event.

Fear kept me from considering the "what if" scenarios back then, and it's what keeps a lot of women from venturing into difficult territory. This is understandable, but it's risky. And it is probably one of the reasons that women remain vulnerable—they fail to acknowledge the strengths and weaknesses of their current situation and to create a plan to give themselves better options. It's simply too complicated or too scary.

I follow the work of Brendan Burchard, and in one of his videos he said something that really struck me: **"Stop trying to get out of the work. Just do it."** Don't complain, don't procrastinate, just do it. There is no such thing as success without doing the work. It may not be fun, but it is necessary, so get on with it and reap the benefits forever more. And as so many of the women I interviewed have said, it *can* be done. Don't let fear stop you from making the right choice for you.

Since Malcolm's death, my approach to life has evolved. I have retained my sense of optimism; I view the universe as an abundant place. The difference now is, while I fully expect the best possible outcome in every area of my life, at the same time I plan for the worst. This does not mean fixating on any potential negative outcomes, it just means acknowledging that they exist and putting a plan in place in the event that they materialize. As soon as the plan is in place, I turn my gaze back to the goal.

Knowing what I know now, here is what I would say to my twenty-something self:

"Continue to love and support Malcolm, but don't let go of your future. You have worked hard to earn your place in the PhD program. It will continue to serve you well both personally and financially, especially if Malcolm is unable to work. Your academic career will be a source of income and stability for you both. Your path is laid out, and you have garnered respect among your peers. Don't walk away from that built-in support.

Malcolm's business must find a way to survive on its own. Joining the business will only delay necessary decisions about ensuring that Malcolm's role is more hands-off when it comes to production. Instead of having a production facility, perhaps he can license the designs to someone else who will develop and sell them internationally. Let Malcolm find a way to develop his graphic talents in a way that will allow him to focus on becoming well. He loves to draw; that's what he should be doing. He should not be doing manual labor. His health isn't up to it, nor is it in his best interests. Whichever way he proceeds, his path is his and his alone to choose. You cannot choose for him.

The last thing you want to be doing is manual labor in a business that isn't yours, that doesn't resonate with any of your goals and aspirations. You have spent all of your adolescent years and early twenties learning to stand on your own two feet. The step you're about to take will make you entirely dependent on Malcolm. Is that really what you want? Is that the right choice for you? You know that it isn't.

You have invested seven years into your university studies and one year overseas. That's valuable, it means something to you, and it is part of the path that you have so carefully selected for yourself. Honor your choices, and help Malcolm to set his path in his own way. It can be done."

If I had chosen to commit to my studies and my future, all other discussions would have flowed from there: where to live, how to manage Malcolm's treatments, what to do about his business, and so forth. The discussions would not have been easy but they would likely have led to a better outcome for us both. Six years later I would certainly not be facing several hundred thousand dollars of debt with no sustainable income.

By failing to take the time to think about my situation and to evaluate the consequences of each potential choice before me, I let circumstances dictate my path. No wonder I wasn't happy with the results.

Think about your own life. Have you thought about the choices you're making—or not making—both big and small? Here's a quick test: Are you where you thought you would be at this point in your life? If not, why not? What happened in the last five or ten years to change the course of your life? Is it a positive change? Has it left you vulnerable in any way? Have you asked all of the uncomfortable "what if" questions outlined earlier?

I realize it's exactly 0% fun to think about all of this stuff, but here's the deal: if you don't make your own choices, life will choose for you, and I can pretty much guarantee you won't be ecstatic about the results.

It can be overwhelming to consider all of these scenarios, and in the face of a daunting task, all too often we procrastinate. So how *do* you move forward with such big questions? The same way you succeed at anything: one step at a time.

I suggest that you start with the single biggest issue for women: money. I'll talk a lot more about money in *Chapter 11: Is It Really All About Money?* but for the moment here are a few questions that I would ask on this topic:

⋄ Do I have my own source of income?

⋄ Would it cover my needs completely if I took my spouse's income out of the equation?

⋄ What would my life look like if he died?

⋄ What would my life look like if we divorced?

⋄ Would the loss or reduction of his income have an impact on my ability to pay the bills?

⬧ Would I have to incur debt?

⬧ If I choose to delay my career for any reason (e.g., to have and/or look after children), what impact will that have on my income or on my future employment prospects?

⬧ What is my plan in all of these instances?

⬧ What can I do to protect myself financially?

Any progress you make on even a single one of these questions has the potential to transform your life.

Now let's consider the three key questions I've learned to ask when I'm doing this kind of work.

1 What's the upside of doing this?

2 What's the downside of doing this?

3 What's the downside if you do nothing?

Suppose you're considering tackling the issue of your income and you currently don't have a source of income, or it's insufficient to cover all of your expenses and savings requirements on its own. Let's look at what your answers might be to the three key questions.

1 **What's the upside of doing this?** You will create options for yourself in the future and you may even improve your current situation by getting creative about growing your income right now.

2 **What's the downside of doing this?** It's not fun and it takes time. It may also be painful to consider negative outcomes or to take a realistic look at where you are today.

❸ What's the downside if you do nothing? Well, if your spouse's income takes a swing downwards or disappears altogether, you're in financial trouble. If he disappears for any reason, you're in even more hot water unless his insurance coverage can see you through to the end of your days after covering your liabilities. If you divorce, insurance won't help you.

I tend to use the three key questions when I find myself procrastinating. Nick Ortner, author of *The Tapping Solution*, puts it this way: if an item has been on your to-do list for two years, you've got a problem! There is a mental block that's preventing you from moving forward and you need to take the time to figure out why you're not addressing that particular area. The three key questions have been very effective at helping to reveal the source of the issues for me.

But what about the issue of time? Every woman I know is terribly busy juggling fourteen balls in the air. How on earth are you supposed to find the time to think with everything going on? There just isn't enough time, and nobody is selling more of it. What do you do?

Here is what I've learned: we find the time for the things that we value. There is always more time to be found. If you have children, think back to the months following your first child's birth. How crazy busy was that? Did you ever look back and wonder what you did with all of the free time you had before you had kids? It probably didn't feel like you had any spare time left at all.

Then you had a second child and became even busier! You dreamed of the free time you had when you had only one child to take care of. In fact, when your parents take one child for the day, it feels like a holiday. Imagine that: only one kid's needs to look after.

Regardless how busy you are or how many projects you have on the go, if I tell you that I'm paying for a two-week holiday for your family down south this winter, you probably won't refuse on the grounds that you can't possibly spare the time. You will move heaven and earth to make it happen. And so it goes with other priorities.

I've said this before, and it's so important that I will say it again: Taking the time on a regular basis to think about your life, the decisions you're making, and where you're headed is critical. Don't make excuses about why it can't happen. Either your life is a priority or it isn't. If you tell yourself that you'll try to make the time, you will fail. I'm going to quote Yoda on this one: "No! Try not! Do or do not. There is no try."

EITHER YOUR LIFE IS A PRIORITY OR IT ISN'T.

Learn from my experience and just do the work.

COVER YOUR ASSETS, PART I

Estate planning is an important and everlasting
gift you can give your family.

— SUZE ORMAN

We all take a million and one precautions in most aspects of our lives—we lock our doors, leave all our contact numbers for the sitter, slather sunscreen on our kids, and check out the road conditions when the weather seems iffy—but do we take the same precautions with our money?

As women, we go to great lengths to protect our loved ones, and yet, with few exceptions, we place ourselves at the bottom of the priority list. This seems especially true about our financial lives.

Consider the following questions: What mechanisms do you have in place to protect yourself and your money? How many of the following items could you check off your list?

⬦ Valid will

⬦ Power of Attorney

⬦ Sufficient insurance

⬦ Strong credit bureau score

⬦ Individual credit cards

⬦ Limited co-signing of loans

⬦ List of all assets and passwords

Before Malcolm died, I had one item on that list: a good credit score. That's it. When he died, I soon discovered the importance of all the other items mentioned above. Let's take a look at them individually.

Valid Will

True or False:

① When you die, it will make no difference for your partner whether you were married or in a common-law relationship when it comes to the transfer of assets.

② Any jointly held assets automatically pass to the survivor with or without a marriage.

③ If you are not married and not on Title, but you have been living with your partner in "your" house for more than three years, you automatically get possession after his death.

④ If the distribution of assets is clearly spelled out in a valid will, there will be no problems with the estate.

I've discovered two interesting things about death. First, it either brings out the best in people or the worst. Second, we are not all equal in death.

We'll look at the answers to the questions above in a second, but let's begin by considering the issue of behavior. Here is what I've seen and experienced personally: in a time of crisis, people you hardly know will fill your freezer, neighbors will cut your lawn, your closest girlfriends will take over with the kids while you try to deal with what just happened, your friend's brother will sell the car you no longer need, a banker will cut you some slack on an upcoming mortgage renewal, and strangers will donate money to help with expenses.

Then there's the other side—the fight over assets, heirlooms, and family photos, and who gets what and who is excluded. Even when there is a will, people manage to find a way to argue about what they feel should have been done for them or left to their progeny. Loved ones discover unexpected inclusions or exclusions in the will, and suddenly feelings are hurt, noses are bent out of shape, and the war is on. Family members who have been getting along reasonably well for decades suddenly stop speaking to one another.

Much of the above could be prevented with a clearly defined will and good communication with the people it will affect.

SHOCKING STATISTICS

We all know wills are important and many of us know of cases where families have been torn apart because of problems with estates. And yet despite this knowledge, a surprising number of us do not have wills even after we get married and have children.

According to a survey released in 2012 by the Lawyers' Professional Indemnity Co. (LawPRO®), more than half of Canadian adults—56%—don't have a signed will. A 2016 survey by LegalWills.ca pegged the number to be even higher—62%. Furthermore, and this is equally troubling, 12% of existing wills are out of date. The numbers are much the same in the United States.

Twenty years ago I was one of those adults. I didn't have children, so I figured it wasn't a big deal if I didn't have a will since Malcolm would get everything in the event of my death and vice versa. There were so many things vying for attention and so little money to go around that we never stopped to consider putting together a will. As it turned out, that posed a serious problem after Malcolm died.

During his last two weeks in hospital, Malcolm was more contemplative than usual. Interspersed with our usual animated conversations were lengthy moments of rare solemnity. During one such moment, Malcolm confessed he had written something in his diary that he wanted me to see. On a blank page, in the middle of the book, he had written simply, "I, Malcolm Gilbertson, being of sound mind, leave everything to my wife Doris. (Signed Malcolm Gilbertson)." That was it. There was no date and nothing else on the page. At the time I was worried Malcolm had given up, so I tried to dismiss it. I'm saddened to say I'm the one who didn't want to discuss the possibility of his death. I wanted to focus on life, not death.

He assured me he hadn't given up—he just felt better having written down his wishes, and he regretted not having done it sooner with a lawyer. He promised to attend to that as soon as he got out of the hospital.

He never left the hospital though, and I was left with a note, not a valid will. Were it not for a friend's father and an act I dub a Fairy Godfather Intervention, many of our assets would have been frozen, and I would have been in deep trouble. The father in question was a lawyer and he helped me to have the note recognized as a valid will.

When did I find out about the need for a will? Shortly after the funeral, when I was handed a death certificate and told to give a copy to my lawyer along with a copy of the will. *Oh God, the will.* The last thing you need to deal with at a time of great stress and emotional duress is another trauma. Discovering there is no valid will feels a lot like a sucker punch when you're already down.

A will wouldn't have changed the fact that I had no money to fall back on after Malcolm died, nor would it have paid off the daunting bills I faced, but it would have made life a lot easier at a difficult time. When you're dealing with massive stress, anything that makes your life easier is a blessing.

THE FIRST BIG LESSON I LEARNED AS A WIDOW WAS THE IMPORTANCE OF HAVING A WILL.

The first big lesson I learned as a widow was the importance of having a will. As one lawyer put it, if you have assets of any kind, you need a will to sort out how they are to be distributed in the event of your death. If there is no will, the law will dictate who gets what, and that will depend on the jurisdiction in which you live.

Now just for fun let's throw in the question of marriage. Common-law spouses are eligible for benefits and are treated as equals after death, right? Wrong.

Obviously the rules will vary depending on where you live and I encourage you to look into the details in your own province or state. You cannot assume common-law spouses are treated the same way as married spouses in the eyes of the law. The following comments apply to my jurisdiction in Ontario, Canada. This will give you an idea of some of the challenges you might face as a common-law spouse.

Let's review the true or false questions above:

1. When you die, it will make no difference for your partner whether you were married or in a common-law relationship when it comes to the transfer of assets. **FALSE.**

The biggest misconception is that common-law spouses have the same rights as married spouses.

When someone dies intestate (without a will) in Ontario, the married spouse gets the first $225,000 of the estate. The rest of it is divided equally between the surviving spouse and the children. However, there is no automatic transference on death to the common-law spouse. First the estate goes to the biological children, then the parents, and, if the latter are deceased, it passes to the siblings.

A common-law spouse would have to bring an application to the court to receive any part of the estate when there is no will and she does not jointly own the assets. At minimum, she will face headaches and significant costs. There is also no guarantee that she will be successful.

THE BEST WAY FOR ANY WOMAN TO PROTECT HERSELF AND TO MAKE LIFE EASIER IN THE EVENT OF HER PARTNER'S DEATH (MARRIED OR COMMON-LAW) IS TO BE ON TITLE. FOR REAL ESTATE PURPOSES, TITLE REFERS TO OWNERSHIP OF THE PROPERTY.

2. Any jointly held assets automatically pass to the survivor with or without a marriage. **TRUE.**

The best way for any woman to protect herself and to make life easier in the event of her partner's death (married or common-law) is to be on title. For real estate purposes, title refers to ownership of the property. She should be on title for the house as a Joint Tenant, jointly own all assets including bank accounts, and be the named beneficiary for investments, pensions, and insurance policies.

When assets are held jointly, they automatically pass to the survivor; you need only to provide a death certificate and some personal information. Also, and this is important, by avoiding the need for Probate you also avoid estate taxes.

3. If you are *not* married and you are *not* on title but you have been living with your partner in "your" house for more than three years, you automatically get possession after his/her death. **FALSE.**

Where assets are held solely in the deceased's name, a will is invaluable. Bank accounts, cars, and investment accounts can then easily pass to the survivor with a will. Without a will, most assets get added to the estate and must go through Probate, a legal process to determine the distribution of assets. Unfortunately, the province or state takes its share by charging a tax on the value of the assets going through Probate. The higher the value, the more tax you pay.

4. If the distribution of assets is clearly spelled out in a valid will, there will be no problems with the estate. **TRUE.**

The whole process can be summarized as follows:

◇ If you're married, you have more legal rights in many jurisdictions.

◇ When you own assets jointly, you get them automatically as the survivor, thus avoiding estate tax.

◇ When you're the beneficiary on an investment, you get it automatically and avoid estate tax.

The smartest thing you can do for yourself when it comes to avoiding hassles and minimizing estate taxes is to ensure that your spouse has a will and that you own everything jointly.

WHAT IF YOU DIE?

We've looked at how to protect yourself if your spouse dies, but what happens if you die? What about your kids and the other people you love? Who will take care of them? Where will the money come from? Who will get the heirloom necklace you inherited from your grandmother? What about the family photos, the special dishes, wedding ring, and the myriad of sentimental and important items filling your house? Who will get those?

THE ONLY WAY YOU CAN ENSURE YOUR WISHES ARE MET IS IF THEY ARE SPELLED OUT EXPLICITLY IN A WILL.

The only way you can ensure your wishes are met is if they are spelled out explicitly in a will.

Let's assume you're convinced a will is essential. Where do you go to get one? Do you really need a lawyer to create a will? Just a few months ago I would have argued that a good lawyer is essential when it comes to preparing a comprehensive will, particularly if you have children or assets. I would have said a will is much more than a piece of paper; it's about the advice you get beforehand. You can't prepare thoroughly if you don't know what questions to ask. Lawyers are trained to know what to ask and how to put together a comprehensive will.

I still believe using a lawyer is an excellent choice. Interview a few, get quotes, and find one with whom you're comfortable. It's a small price to pay—usually only six to eight hundred dollars—for such a critical document.

That said, I have come across an online service that has made me rethink my bias against such services. Every online DIY will service I've looked at in the past has left me unimpressed. However, a colleague recently pointed me to the website www.LegalWills.ca. I was so intrigued

I called up the president of the company, Tim Hewson, to have a chat about the product. What I discovered impressed me.

After a few telephone conversations and email exchanges with Tim, I decided to give his online services a test-run. Since I already had a will and power of attorney created by a lawyer, I wanted to go through the process at LegalWills.ca and compare the outcome with my "real" will and power of attorney. I fully expected the online result to be far inferior to the documents produced by our lawyer. It was not.

I went through each will line by line to do a comparison and, to my surprise, the online version was similar to my existing will. As might be expected, the latter allowed for more customization but the LegalWills.ca version covered all of the important information. What's more, it guided me through the document in a user-friendly, easy-to-follow manner, and I was done in twenty minutes. To be fair, my husband and I had already thought about all of the difficult issues surrounding the loss of one or both of us, which left me free to simply replicate our choices on the online site. Still, the ease and the quality of the experience impressed me.

There was one area I initially thought would be problematic: in our existing will my husband and I outline what happens in the event that our children predecease us and don't leave any heirs behind. The LegalWills.ca version certainly allowed us to name beneficiaries in that case, but it was a bit more limited in allowing us to explore multiple possibilities. When I brought this up with Tim, he made a great point: **a will should apply to your life right now and should be updated at regular intervals or as your life circumstances change.** It shouldn't be a once-and-done kind of document in which you try to imagine every possible eventuality. For example, our children are currently thirteen and ten. Why on earth would we consider their children when that possibility is (we hope) many years away? By his reasoning we should revise our will many times before our children become parents.

As I thought about what he said, I realized most people, if they have a will at all, produce only one or two wills in their lifetime because of the cost. If a document costs several hundred dollars to produce, you're not going to want to do it every time something changes in your life. Yet that's precisely what you should do in order to ensure it's up to date.

Which is easier, trying to foresee the future or revising your will every time there is a major change in your life? (e.g., the birth of a child, the death of a family member, a change in key friendships.)

Tim has addressed the concern over prohibitive costs by charging $39.95 (at time of printing) for a will and ($29.95) for a power of attorney with unlimited updates free of charge. That's compelling. In my case, my husband and I paid more than $600 for a will and powers of attorney. If we want to make any changes, we have to pay our lawyer his standard rate of $225/hour. The same documents through LegalWills.ca would have cost us less than $150 with the possibility of unlimited updates. We can then pay to have them stored online through LegalWills for $25 for five years or up to $125 for a lifetime, with many other price points in between.

I have become a big fan of LegalWills.ca, as I think it takes money out of the equation—and off the list of excuses—for virtually everyone. There is no good reason not to have a will, especially given the availability of a service like LegalWills.ca. (American and British versions are also available.)

Does that mean you should not go to a lawyer? No, it does not. In my case, my husband and I have a corporation and a portfolio of properties to consider, which goes beyond the mandate of an online will service. For anyone with a business or complex holdings, it is worth getting a separate will done by a lawyer to address all of those assets. Similarly, if you have a complex personal situation (e.g., a child with special needs) a lawyer's advice is invaluable. For everyone else though, it's hard to argue with the value proposition offered by LegalWills.

I have worked out a discount code for my readers: THRIVE20. If you're interested in using LegalWills.ca, simply go to their website and use my discount code—THRIVE20—to receive a 20% discount. It's an affiliate link in which we both share in the savings. I will donate my 15% commission to women's shelters in Ottawa. Win-win.

POWER OF ATTORNEY

A Power of Attorney is a legal document that gives someone else the right to act on your behalf. With this document in place, if your spouse becomes incapacitated or is unable to make financial decisions about selling assets held wholly or partly in his name, you are legally empowered to act on their behalf.

In my jurisdiction, there are two kinds of power of attorney: Continuing Power of Attorney for property and Power of Attorney for personal care.

The former applies to assets whereas the latter applies when a person is no longer able to make medical decisions regarding his or her care. These documents allow you to choose a person you trust to make difficult decisions for you and to respect your wishes.

If something happens to your spouse to render him mentally incapable, you want to have the documents you need to be able to respond quickly and effectively. Do this as soon as possible. Once again, you can obtain them through a lawyer or through a reputable service like LegalWills.ca. If you use the latter, remember to use my discount code, THRIVE20, to receive a 20% discount.

In my case, I was lucky Malcolm's doctors allowed me to make decisions about his care even without a Power of Attorney in place. Recall how doctors turned to me when it became clear there was no hope for Malcolm. I made the decision to unplug his life-support system. If his parents or siblings had disagreed with my decision, I could potentially have had a problem. With no Power of Attorney in place, I wouldn't have had the authority to make decisions on Malcolm's behalf in the face of disputes on how best to proceed.

Do yourself a big favor: put these legal documents in place for you and your spouse without delay.

10

DIVORCE

TAHANI

What would you do if you came home from school at fifteen years of age only to be told by your family that, surprise, you're now married and will move to Canada with your new husband within a few months?

That is precisely what happened to Tahani. I've interviewed a number of women with exceptional stories, but Tahani's life story is one of the most challenging I've heard.

Tahani was born in a refugee camp in Jordan. While life in the camp was hardly lavish, she and her family managed to survive reasonably well. If we considered her early life by Canadian standards, we would be shocked. Decades later, even her own children were taken aback the first time they went over for a visit, yet Tahani had never felt poor or diminished during her childhood.

Her life took a sharp turn in February of 1981 when she learned of her fate. By August of that year, she was in Canada with a new husband whom she barely knew. Suddenly she was a married woman in a new country, learning a new language, having to attend to her house and husband while going to school like other kids her age.

As Tahani explains, she was naive and felt she had to do what was expected of her culturally. It was not an easy situation. Twenty-two years later, Tahani knew the marriage had to end, not for her sake but for her kids. She packed up her children and left with little money to her name.

She then had a new and pressing problem. They needed a roof over their heads and money to live on. Sometime earlier she had become a realtor and had experienced the ups and downs of the business, but every time she started to see some success, she would sabotage it. That, in part, is what kept her in the marriage so long: she didn't believe she could make it on her own.

This time, however, she simply *had* to succeed. Her first act was to purchase a semi-detached house with the help of a banker who believed in her. Tahani was terrified. Two kids, no financial support, no real income, and now a house to pay for—who wouldn't be scared!

The banker's act of faith and kindness gave her courage. A few months later, after sinking to a low point financially and emotionally, she made a decision. She would prove to her husband she could do it on her own, because there was no way she was going back.

She started knocking on doors and asking builders for their business. "I wasn't shy about telling people I needed the work to feed my kids and that I was willing to work very hard to do whatever it took to sell or buy homes for my clients. People are amazing. They want to help. They also respond to your desire to go the extra mile for them and get the job done. Clients believed me and they gave me a chance. I started getting great results."

Four and a half years later, Tahani had purchased nine other houses in addition to paying off the mortgage for her semi-detached home. When I asked how she did it, she replied, "I would take my kids to sports, to school, and work, work, work. I slept very little and worked like a mad woman non-stop. There was no dating or leisure time. I was focused and committed to doing whatever it took to take care of my kids. I got creative and didn't spend money on *anything!* I just put money in the bank. For the first year and a half I wouldn't even buy a $1.10 cup of coffee! I had a plan and I stuck to it."

Tahani has since developed a multimillion-dollar real estate portfolio and has branched out into large real estate development projects as both a developer and an investor. She has become a best-selling author as well as an international speaker who helps others accomplish their dreams.

Needless to say, she has a lot of advice for women:

⬦ Be courageous. Face your money situation. Know what's happening with your money. Don't be naive. Whether you want to or not, you will have to face it at some point.

⬦ You don't need to know everything before acting. Action is a great way to learn.

⬦ Manage your own money. Understand money and how it works. When women give away their money power to their spouses or anyone else, they set themselves up to become victims. Women need to understand what is happening and be responsible for their decisions and their wealth.

⬦ Believe you can do it. You have something important to bring to the table. Develop self-confidence by taking small, consistent steps. Every single step forward builds your wins.

⬦ Don't look for excuses. If you want it badly enough, you'll do it. For Tahani, it was initially about providing for her kids. Now it's about contribution. Understand what is driving you, what your "why" is.

⬦ Understand your relationship to money—are you a saver, spender, avoider? What do you think of when you see money? What are your feelings about money? Write down your answers and understand what is behind those emotions.

⬥ Focus on the people you can help. Life is about adding value to others. Money is a by-product; it comes to you because you seek to help.

⬥ Focusing on building your future is as important as reducing debt. Think future and think investments. Come up with wealth-creation ideas, and then save and invest.

⬥ Life has ups and down, but you'll be OK. Any woman is capable of doing whatever she wants. Even if you cannot see how to accomplish a goal, do the actions and have faith. It takes work to be successful. You must be committed. Be courageous and step out of your comfort zone.

DIANA

You can never tell what lies beneath a person's exterior. My friend Diana is a great example of this. She is positive, engaging, grounded, and strong. I had no idea what she had been through until I interviewed her for this project.

When Diana heard I was working on a book to help women, she told me to grab a glass of wine, sit down, and listen. She had a story to tell.

Jeffrey was a firefighter and a ladies' man throughout his twenties and early thirties. Apparently there was quite a revolving door of women entering and exiting his life in quick succession. His sister eventually decided that, since Jeff was doing such a poor job of picking women, she would select a great girl for him. She felt at his age, it was time for him to calm down and grow up. She introduced Diana to Jeff in 1994, and they instantly clicked.

Diana and Jeff were happy, independent, social people, and it worked out brilliantly for a number of years. He loved to cook; she loved to entertain. Neither of them liked conflict, so when issues arose, they would cool off and calmly discuss the problems afterwards. To everyone's delight, Jeff seemed to have settled down into a happy life with Diana, who had moved into his house within the first year.

As Diana came to know Jeff, she learned of his horrific childhood. His mother used to beat the kids and, when Jeff was eight years old, he witnessed his father kill his mother and his grandmother. His father went to prison for the double murder, but after five years he was released for "good behavior." As far as Diana could see, Jeff seemed to have dealt with that terrible past and had developed into a positive person with a successful career.

Roughly one year after they became a couple, they decided to invest in a business together with a few other partners. Diana already had a health-services practice, but she felt this would be a great opportunity for growth. Thus she became a minority shareholder in the enterprise.

In the early days, cash flow was a significant issue for their enterprise, resulting in multiple cash calls. Jeff took out a second mortgage on his house and he asked Diana to sign the papers, claiming it would give her partial ownership. According to Diana, this is where she made her first critical mistake: she signed the documents without reviewing them carefully or questioning Jeff. He was her life partner. Why wouldn't she trust him?

By the year 2000, things were beginning to change for Diana and Jeff. Diana's father had died and left her some cash as well as his Lexus. Diana used the money to buy a cottage at a ski resort, a place that would become a refuge for her. Meanwhile, Jeff used the car as collateral for one of his loans.

Around the same time, Jeff's father died. Given the family history, Diana expected the news would bring some closure for Jeff, but instead it seemed to trigger a deep, emotional reaction. Jeff began to withdraw and become reclusive, just as he had done in his early twenties. He would disappear for as long as a week without any word or indication of his whereabouts. Colleagues and family alike were beside themselves with worry and couldn't believe he hadn't said a word to Diana. Diana was shocked by his behavior.

When Jeff returned home, he would refuse to discuss where he had been, what he had done, and why he had left. Diana would become upset and insist they needed to talk, but instead of addressing his behavior, he would disappear again. Faced with an untenable situation, Diana suggested to Jeff that they get counseling.

"I don't have a problem; you're the one with the problem," he said.

"OK, I'm the one with the problem. Let's go to counseling to see what I can do about it then."

Jeff refused and kicked her out of his house when it became clear Diana wasn't going to leave things alone.

Diana was reluctant to leave, even despite the insistence of Jeff's family and friends that she go in order to protect herself. She was in shock and in denial. "It will get better. He needs help." But they'd all had long experience in dealing with him and insisted she leave.

As Diana explains, she didn't plan her departure very well because she believed they still had a chance. At first, she slept on the sofa at a friend's house until she could get her head together. Then she moved four times in a period of one year. Since her health practice had been located in Jeff's house, she now had to relocate her business. Unfortunately, the resulting disruption had a big impact on her clientele.

After Diana left, Jeff became nasty and vindictive. He stopped paying the loan for which the car was collateral, and eventually Diana's father's car was repossessed. Diana then faced another shock when she discovered that, despite nine years together and a document which she believed gave her a share of the house, she in fact owed money for a second mortgage and other business loans. Years earlier, Jeff had asked her to sign a document which he implied would give her 50% ownership of the house, when in fact it was a loan agreement. Diana signed the document without verifying it because she trusted Jeff. She had no idea she was signing a loan document.

It didn't end there. Jeff went after her for half of the cottage, Diana's sole place of refuge and, at the time, her only residence. Thankfully a judge rebuked Jeff for the latter move and suggested that if Diana took the matter to trial, she would walk away with a lot more than just her cottage. Jeff quickly backed down.

It was clear Jeff was out to destroy her, but what could she do? She had signed on the dotted line for a variety of loans. A lawyer recommended she get a loan to pay out her share of the debts and thereby get Jeff out of her life officially. By the time the matter was resolved, Diana had lost her father's car and had incurred $60,000 of debt.

The hardest part of the whole experience for Diana was the loss of her profession. "How could I go on pretending to be a healer when I was completely broken inside? Jeff had destroyed my soul. I needed to repair and rebuild myself before I could think of helping someone else. I also desperately needed money to live, so I had no choice but to find a job in another industry." Diana found a job with a government policing agency as their communications specialist, a field she works in to this day.

"Doris, I've learned so much over the years. I've got a long list of advice for women"

Take it from Diana.

⬦ Never sign a document you don't understand. It is fine to trust someone, but always verify anything that you're about to sign. Have a lawyer review it and explain it to you. It's much cheaper to do that than to pay for it afterwards.

⬧ Do not tell your spouse you're leaving until you've discussed your situation with a lawyer and friends, and you've found a place to live. Ensure you are secure and that you have your circle of experts and supports in place.

⬧ Go for what is fair and fight back to defend what is rightfully yours. Be strategic.

⬧ Don't assume that a breakup will be amicable. I made that mistake and I got burned. Protect yourself.

⬧ Choose a lawyer before you leave, before you're desperate, and choose the lawyer you want. I took what I could afford and that hurt me. In the end I would have benefited by hiring a better lawyer.

⬧ Always review your own documents. Jeff did my taxes for years, and afterwards I discovered he had lied to the government about a number of things for his benefit. My accountant and I went to Revenue Canada to declare the problem afterwards, but it caused me a ton of stress and worry about what the possible repercussions. Take responsibility for your own documents.

⬧ Never stay angry or sit at home wondering who your ex is with. I learned that Jeff had been having an affair at the end of our relationship, and within three weeks of my departure someone else moved in. If you stay angry and bitter, you allow them to control you. Go for therapy, go dancing, do sports, do creative things—whatever you need to do to allow your strength and clarity to surface once again. Leave the past in the past and embrace the freedom that comes with that.

◇ Forgive yourself for any mistakes you made. I was so ashamed that I had "lost" my father's car and that I had not taken better care of it. It felt like I had betrayed my parents. My sister put it into perspective for me: "It's just a car." I needed to forgive myself. We all make mistakes. Move on, learn, and don't let it happen to you again.

IS IT REALLY ALL ABOUT MONEY?

Money isn't everything,
but it is right up there with oxygen.

— Trish Schwenkler

Have you ever thought about the part that money plays in your life? Naturally we all know money is needed to live, and most of us spend a great many of our days working to sustain our families. So sure, money is necessary, but just *how* necessary is it?

As it turns out, money has a profound effect on most key areas of our lives.

Let's start by taking a look at the impact on our health. The statistics on poverty are pretty sobering. The World Health Organization has declared that poverty is the single largest determinant of health. Kids who grow up in poor families have worse health outcomes than kids who come from higher socio-economic households.

You might counter that, while these statistics hold for families living in poverty, you're doing just fine right now, even in a low-income state. Perhaps. But this is where my "what if" questions come into play. If your income continues and no one ever gets sick, then you may be fine. If life happens though, you may be in trouble if you have no financial buffer to fall back on.

What about happiness? Does a lack of money have a big impact? You could argue that many families are happy despite being poor. My own parents used to say this to me all the time when I was growing up: "You don't need money to be happy." They would use my father's family as an example—they had many kids, little money, and lots of joy. While I agree you can have fun and experience joy without having a dime to your name, it is nonetheless easier to be happy when you do have money.

As a kid, whenever I heard the line about not needing money to be happy, I'd think the adults were using it as justification for their own situation. I didn't buy it for a minute. These are the same people who started work early in life to the detriment of their educations in order to help support their families. They made huge sacrifices because of financial hardship. I admire them, and I'm proud of what they have accomplished with so few resources in their early years, but theirs is hardly an enviable path.

It's also true that money challenges are at the root of many arguments between married couples. The Office for National Statistics in the UK quantified the problem: "Money worries were reported as the main factor that puts a strain on a relationship by 62% of people aged 16 and over in the UK in 2014."

When I look back at my time with Malcolm, all of our arguments boiled down to a single cause: money. What appeared to be an argument about a health-related matter was at its core an issue about a lack of money and the resulting lack of options. Some treatments were out of reach for us because we couldn't afford them. What should we do then?

Each compromise added to our stress levels, which in turn compounded every other problem. It can be a vicious circle.

MONEY YIELDS OPTIONS

If you have money, you have options. Do you need more time with your family? You plan a holiday because you can afford it. Do you need expensive medicines or treatments to deal with a medical issue? Or do you just need time off to heal? No problem, you can afford it. Do you want to expose your kids to quality educational opportunities? Sign them up for camps and extra-curricular activities because you have the funds to do so. Does a family member need help to get through a rough time? You take time off because you can afford to.

While no one could maintain that money is the most important factor in people's lives, it is indeed right up there with oxygen. It may not be a sufficient condition for health and happiness, but it appears to be an important one.

I grew up in a family that had little money. I had a happy childhood with many great experiences, but I was also keenly aware of our limited resources. I felt the absence of certain luxuries other kids had. When I became a teenager, I resolved to never again be a have-not. I have since been broke, and I also know what it's like to live an abundant lifestyle. I can tell you which I'd recommend.

So why am I talking about this? It boils down to the importance for women to understand how money works and to grow their net worth so they are protected regardless of what happens. I failed to do this in my twenties and I paid a heavy price.

From the moment I abandoned my PhD, money was an issue. While Malcolm's business grew rapidly, generating a respectable amount of cash, there were also a lot of expenses involved in growing the company and establishing the operations. In addition, Malcolm's medical costs were considerable. As self-employed people in Canada, we had no medical plan; we had to pay for many of Malcolm's medications and other costs associated with his treatments.

Prior to this, I had been a saver and an investor. Granted, back then my investment choices were not sophisticated, but they nevertheless helped to move me forward financially. My income was rising and the future looked bright. And then cancer came along.

One of our big problems was that we never discussed money or the future. Looking back, I can see how it happened. Malcolm wasn't sure he would have a future. What's the point of having five-year goals when your doctors keep telling you that you'll be a dead man before that? For me, the future seemed to vanish; there was only today. Today we need to get to an appointment. Today we need to deal with another pressing business concern. Today we need to pay bills. We'd get to the rest tomorrow. The problem of course, is that tomorrow never came.

I now realize what a mistake it was to forget about the future. By not thinking about financing my future, and by not having a "what if" fund, I set myself up for hardship when Malcolm died. Not only was my income threatened by his death, as I discussed in the last chapter, but I also had no net worth to help me get through the aftermath of losing him. No financial resources equals no options. I couldn't take the time to properly grieve when a financial crisis loomed ahead. Even the cost of the funeral posed a real problem.

IT WAS A HORRIBLE EXPERIENCE AND KNOWING WHAT I KNOW NOW, I HAVE MADE DEVELOPING A STRONG NET WORTH A PRIORITY. HAVING MONEY, AND MORE SPECIFICALLY, OPTIONS, REALLY IS A BIG DEAL.

When Malcolm died, we had just paid for much of the business stock required for the Christmas retail season. Plus, Malcolm spent the last month and a half of his life in the hospital. Prior to that he had been unable to do much for nearly seven months. Our business productivity had all but ground to a halt and, with little money coming in, the coffers began to empty.

If you have a buffer and net worth to turn to, you can ride out a crisis and pay for services to help you through. Without the cash, you're stuck and your options are bleak. It was a horrible experience and knowing what I know now, I have made developing a strong net worth a priority. Having money, and more specifically, options, really is a big deal.

CONTROL OVER YOUR FINANCIAL FUTURE

Fast forward ten years. I have become a real estate investor and have created a rent-to-own company that helps families sort out their credit issues as part of the process of buying their own home. A key element of my work entails looking at people's credit reports and talking to them about their financial lives. After reviewing hundreds of files, an interesting trend has emerged: women are typically the money managers of the family. They pay the bills, plan the family's expenditures, and manage the day-to-day household finances. However, they don't often get involved in long-term financial planning or investing, relying instead on their spouses to take the lead on this front.

In light of what I've just told you about my own experience, do you see a problem with this? We're not talking about uneducated women either. I have spoken to women with graduate degrees, executives in large companies, entrepreneurs running six-figure businesses, and women in the financial sector. These ladies are smart, successful, and capable, yet the vast majority of them abdicate responsibility for their financial futures to their husbands.

One conversation in particular stands out. The woman I was speaking with—let's call her Amy—told me she earns six figures working in a leadership position in a prominent government department. By her own estimation, she is a confident person. However, when her family's financial planner comes over, she lets her husband do all the talking. He also makes the decisions because, as she puts it, she feels like an idiot. "I don't understand a thing the planner says. It's like he's speaking a foreign language." When I asked her why she doesn't ask him questions to clarify the points he's making, she says she's too embarrassed. She doesn't want him to know the extent of her ignorance on the topic so she just nods, agrees with her husband, and says nothing.

"Do you know what holdings you have and the value of the portfolio?" I asked.

"No. I know some of the companies that show up on the statements, but I don't understand how it all works. I can read the overall value at the bottom of the statement, but I know little beyond that. Honestly, I rarely read the statements. My husband looks after it all."

In short, she has little control over her financial future. So she must be handing over the reins to her husband because he's well-versed in investing, right? Not at all. He apparently understands to some extent how stocks and mutual funds work, but he spends no time on the investments beyond discussing the portfolio with the financial planner on an annual basis. That's not a rock-solid strategy, particularly when you consider the statistics on the average performance of financial planners. The vast majority (i.e., 96%) of them fail to beat the market. Some planners are excellent, but you won't know until you understand what they're doing and how to evaluate their performance.

I get where Amy's coming from. That was me in my twenties—except the bit about earning six figures. Many intelligent, educated women are either giving total control to their husbands on the assumption he will make better investment choices, or they put it off until "later" because they are too busy managing their family life. The problem, as we've seen, is that later never comes.

Beat the Market: Beating the market means to earn a return on investment that is greater than that of the S&P 500 index, one of the most popular benchmarks of the U.S. stock market performance, or the return of the Dow Jones Industrial Average index. There are many ways to calculate the market average, but usually a benchmark like the S&P 500 or the Dow Jones is used as they are a reasonably good representation of the market average. When a financial advisor fails to beat the market, it means that their funds, or fund choices, have yielded lower returns than a simple index fund tracking the S&P 500 or the Dow Jones Industrial Average index.

Back in the 1960s, a *Leave it to Beaver* Cleaver-like distribution of familial responsibility was the norm. Men earned the money and took care of the investments while women looked after the house and the children. Fifty years later however, the world is a different place. We are starting to realize we can't afford to give up control of our future. It behooves us to educate ourselves about this fundamental aspect of our lives and take responsibility for creating a money plan and see it through.

WE ARE STARTING TO REALIZE WE CAN'T AFFORD TO GIVE UP CONTROL OF OUR FUTURE.

It's important to note that none of the men I have spoken to has tried to exclude his wife from the investment process. *Women* shy away from getting involved. Men aren't doing this to us; by and large, we're choosing to keep ourselves in the dark.

If we want to be cynical about it, we can look at it in this way: on average, women outlive men, therefore every woman will be faced with making decisions about investments at some point in her life. Toss in the statistics on divorce and it looks like a lot more women are going to have to figure it out sooner rather than later. And I can tell you from experience that it's a lot easier to deal with challenging issues before a crisis than during or after one. If you think you don't have time to figure it out now, just wait until a challenge hits. Then you'll be wondering why on earth you didn't tackle this sooner.

Let's apply the three key questions to the assertion that you should develop a money plan and grow your net worth.

- ① **What's the upside of creating a money plan and growing my net worth?** I will strengthen my financial position (which is a form of protection), create options for myself in the event that something unforeseen happens, and I will grow my self-confidence in a key area of my life. This is a big win for me and it's a win for my family as they will also benefit from improvements to my financial health.

- ② **What's the downside of doing this?** I will feel overwhelmed and clueless. I don't know where to start or who to believe. I'm also afraid of making mistakes. What if I lose money? And how will I find the time to get all of this done? I'm maxed out as it is.

- ③ **What's the downside of doing nothing?** If I don't have a financial buffer and a reasonable net worth, I am vulnerable and so are my children. If something changes in our family's income or if someone develops a health issue, we could be in trouble. In addition, if my spouse leaves me or dies, I would be left in a difficult position on top of having to deal with emotional trauma.

The risks associated with not having financial resources to weather a storm are significant. There is a huge payoff, to being financially strong. So why aren't more women tackling this? The answer revolves around a fear of losing money and a lack of confidence.

Sandra Tisiot, a mortgage specialist, and I recently conducted a survey in order to determine in which area women feel the least confident when it comes to finances. Was it knowing how to protect themselves legally? Managing money on a day-to-day basis? Investing? Developing and maintaining a good credit score? Interestingly, an overwhelming majority of the respondents stated that investing posed the biggest challenge for them and that they felt most confident managing money on a day-to-day basis. That is entirely consistent with what I've seen in my rent-to-own business and with what I routinely hear from women at speaking engagements.

In her excellent book *Shortchanged: Why Women Have Less Wealth and What Can Be Done About It,* Mariko Lin Chang, former Associate Professor of Sociology at Harvard University, explores the reasons behind the significant wealth gap between men and women. In part, we behave very differently when it comes to investing. Here is a quick overview of her findings:

◈ Men and women have a different perception of risk.

◈ Women are more likely to view lost money as irreplaceable.

◈ Men have a greater sense of confidence about their ability to make money.

◈ However, research shows women often perform better than men when making investment decisions.

⬨ Despite this, women still shy away from getting involved in investments.

The wealth gap will continue until women do something about it. We should care deeply about this because this affects our vulnerability and our ability to bounce back in the face of adversity.

I completely understand it can be daunting to tackle the issue of investments, particularly if you're dealing with debt and struggling to stay on top of the bills every month. In March of 2014, *TIME* Magazine reported that nearly half of North Americans live paycheck to paycheck. This is clearly a big problem. The fastest way out of that problem is to stop, take stock, create a plan, and focus on the priorities. Growing our hard-earned money and making it work for us is a priority.

If you're ready to start creating your money plan and tackle investments, take a look at my Facebook page, www.facebook.com/SurviveThriveandGrow, as well as my website www.dorisbelland.com. You'll find free resources, blog posts, and tools to help you. Look out for upcoming workshops on investing geared specifically to women.

One final thought about investing: it won't get easier until you tackle it. Remember the saying, "The way to eat an elephant is one bite at a time." There are many resources to help you. As you move through the process, remind yourself that there is no such thing as a stupid question. You are learning, so cut yourself some slack. No one learns anything of value without asking questions and making mistakes. Lots of them. If you've lost money in the past, so what? Let it go. Leave the past where it belongs—behind you. Your past should not define your future.

TACKLING A MOUNTAIN OF DEBT

Debt is an ingenious substitute for the
chain and whip of the slave driver.

— AMBROSE BIERCE

How do you move forward when you're under a big pile of debt? That's the question I faced when I first emerged from the grief-induced fog after Malcolm's death. I had a six-figure mortgage as well as six-figure business debt. With a bit of luck, I had a two-year runway of income before the business died. The pressure was on to find a solution.

Life is full of ironic twists. Today, in my rent-to-own business, most of the client files that come across my desk reveal credit issues in which debt features prominently as the culprit. So when clients tell me they're overwhelmed with debt, I understand where they're coming from. I've been there. The reasons for my debt may be different than most, but debt is debt. You have to tackle it before you can move forward with your life, particularly if the debt is corrosive, as with credit card or consumer debt.

Thankfully, I did not have credit card debt, due in large part to my father's influence. My dad is a cash kind of guy. When I was growing up, I kept hearing the same thing over and over again: Buy only what you can pay for. If you don't have the money, start saving, and wait to make the purchase. I'm pretty sure my dad was in his sixties before he had a credit card and you can bet it gets paid in full every single month.

To my young, inexperienced mind, debt was a bad thing. It got people into trouble and caused nothing but grief. As I grew older, I began to understand that debt was necessary to grow a business and to buy a house, but for all other purchases I insisted on having the cash in hand first.

I'm deeply grateful to my father for that lesson. As bad as my financial situation was after Malcolm died, it could have been a lot worse if I had followed the societal norm of using credit cards as a cash-flow tool to fund consumer purchases. Instead, I had business debt and a house that I could no longer afford to keep.

WRITE IT DOWN AND BREATHE

The first step I took, after the shock wore off, was to make a list of all of my debts. I needed to know how much was owed, to whom, and when it needed to be paid off. My stress level rose as I listed line after line of debt, but I kept telling myself to breathe. I would figure it out. At one point I remember walking away from the list thinking I couldn't take any more. I went for another pavement-pounding walk and, when I had calmed down, returned to my list. I knew I needed to know the full extent of the problem before starting on a solution. You can't solve a problem if you can't stare it in the face to begin with.

The mortgage on the house was the least of my concerns since the rate was good and I still had a couple years left on the term. I would tackle that last. The first hurdle was the business debt. Some of it came in the form of credit with our suppliers, as we had purchased all of the supplies for the all-important Christmas retail season, but none of it had been transformed into final consumer goods.

I had a choice: I could ask the suppliers for a 30–60 day extension so I had time to prepare the products and sell them. Or, I could order even more product and double up our sales efforts to bring in as much cash as possible.

GO FOR THE BIG WINS

It was a big bet, but I had only two years to make all of the money I needed to pay my bills or face bankruptcy. I needed a bold move. I called our suppliers and I worked out a deal. I would order twice as much product, but I needed twice the amount of time to pay them back. In the end, they would get more sales and I would get the time I needed to put more sales channels into place.

The reason this worked is that I was honest with my suppliers. They knew Malcolm had died and I was candid about my determination to maximize sales over the next two years to pay off debt. They also knew we had established markets to sell our product. I had always paid my bills on time before and I had also built a great working relationship with the suppliers. Thankfully, it paid off and they agreed.

Then I sat down to brainstorm every conceivable way to sell our products. I made deals with stores, offered incentives to our buyers, and doubled up on the retail consumer shows in which we participated. I reached out to friends who needed more cash and I hired them as temporary sales people.

PAY OFF EXPENSIVE DEBT FIRST

It was exhausting and stressful, but it worked. That Christmas I doubled our usual sales. I paid back all of our suppliers, and with the extra cash, I started to pay off bank loans. I began with the most expensive loans, wiped those out, and then tackled the remaining debt.

Once the Christmas season was over, I immediately got to work planning other ways to generate sales during the typically slow winter period. I put our products in every conceivable outlet and personally participated in any sales opportunity I could find.

A not-for-profit was having an event, and they loved our stuff, so I set up a booth and split the profits with them. I even set up a booth at a Star Trek convention despite being as far removed from a Trekkie as you can imagine. It was a bizarre experience, but it brought in more cash, and that's all I cared about at the time. The whole time I was at the convention though, I kept asking myself, "What the hell are you doing here?" Especially when one committed Trekkie took a shining to me and starting showing up every day with treats, including a quart of Häagen-Dazs ice cream. Then I'd remind myself, "You're here to pay off your debt. Shut up and smile." I thanked him, tried to gently hint I was not looking for a new mate, and counted the seconds until I could disappear.

SELL UNUSED ITEMS

In between events, I evaluated every personal and business item I owned. If I had not used it in the last year, I sold it. Clothes, furniture, kitchen appliances, production equipment, art supplies, tools—everything that could be sold, went. Every dime that I earned from those sales went to paying down debt.

Then there was the matter of the house. Before I could list the place, I needed to sell all of the equipment stored in the garage and basement. We had a massive collection of tools courtesy of Malcolm's propensity for impromptu purchases of sales items, so I made an inventory and reached out to everyone I could think of, friend or business colleague, with a sales list. I sold all but an essential collection of tools, which I kept for myself. Some people drove four to five hours to come scoop up some bargains. All the while, the stock of items kept going down.

During one of my evening walks, it occurred to me that farmers might be interested in some of the stuff I had for sale. I drew up a list for them and dropped it off to every mailbox within a mile radius of my house. It was quite time-consuming, but I ended up selling most of the items on my list.

As I thought about listing the house for sale, I knew I would have to make some major changes. To put it mildly, the house was ugly. The lot was beautiful, but there was nothing redeeming about the structures. I had never liked the place. Malcolm, on the other hand, had loved it.

"But Doris," Malcom would say, "there's a massive garage and a ton of space inside the house, not to mention more than two acres of land. We would have our own woods in the back. We can have tea or wine in our back yard while watching the birds. It's perfect! And it's cheap compared to the properties in town."

"Cheaper, yes, but we'd be twenty minutes away from decent food shops, and the place is a seventies nightmare. Is there anything uglier than a multilevel, split A-frame? And did you notice the inside? 'Dated' doesn't even begin to cover it."

"That's superficial. We can change that."

Except we didn't. Malcolm died fifteen months after we bought the house. I was left with a dated, ugly house in the country.

WORK WITH WHAT YOU'VE GOT

What's the most important factor in buying real estate? That's right, location, location, location. Strike number one against the house. There was nothing I could do about the location, so I would have to improve the curb appeal and the inside.

Ron and I set to work updating the house on the inside. One of the biggest issues with the house was how the front door opened directly into the living room. There was no room to move on the tiny landing, and there was no closet. It was a completely daft setup, and from the very start, Malcolm and I had intended to move the front door to a tiny room ten feet to the left. The room was barely big enough for an office; it would make a far better foyer with room for a proper closet.

Ron and I looked into the cost of adding a window in the living room where the door was and bricking in the outside. When we discovered it would be a relatively inexpensive project, we got to work.

There was a strange moment at Home Depot when I rented the jackhammer to destroy the concrete steps. The fellow working the Rental desk kept asking me if my husband would be by to pick it up so he could talk to him about how to use it. I insisted I would be the one taking it home and using it, as my husband was indisposed. I got that sort of thing a lot from contractors as I rented various large tools to complete the renovations. It was a moment of personal victory for me when I showed up at the house and presented Ron with the jackhammer. We took turns chipping away the resistant concrete steps.

It took several months to get the property ready for sale, but when it was all prepped, I couldn't wait to get out of there. Everything about that house had a negative association for me—loss, heartache, constant work, isolation. I was done with it.

In the end, it took two listing agents, seventeen months, and a new roof to sell the property for roughly the same price we had paid for it. The sale would represent an overall loss for me. When you factor in what I had spent on renovations, legal fees, and realtor fees with no appreciation in value to offset those expenditures, it amounted to a loss on paper. I didn't care about the loss, though; I just wanted the place gone. I knew there was enough equity from our initial down payment to yield a bit of a check at the end of the process, and that's all I wanted. Every month I owned the place was costing me money; the closing date couldn't come soon enough for me. I eventually used the money from the sale to pay down the mortgage on the first house that Mark and I bought in Ottawa.

During the two-year process of paying off my debt, I spent virtually nothing on myself. There were no trips, no restaurant meals, and no superfluous expenditures of any kind. I wouldn't even buy myself a cup of coffee. If I could make it more cheaply at home, then buying it was out of the question. This was not a fun time in my life, but it got the job done. Within two years I had eliminated nearly $400,000 of debt.

The day that I paid off the last loan and scratched off the final entry on the list of debts, I remember sitting in the middle of my mostly empty family room looking out at the back yard. I did not feel joy. Malcolm was gone and my life was a shambles. How could I feel joy? I did, however, feel profound relief, and that feeling alone made the effort worthwhile.

If you look back at the women's stories I have shared with you, you will see similar tales of resilience in the face of financial hardship. The common factor in all of our stories is that we had a worthwhile goal and were determined to succeed. When you've left your husband, have no income, and are alone with children to care for, you can accomplish miracles. When you face financial ruin because of a mountain of debt, you suddenly become very creative.

BREAK IT DOWN

If you find yourself in a dire situation financially, I suggest that you start by breaking down the problem into steps. Put it all down on paper—every last, ugly detail. Don't omit anything. Once you have the full extent of the challenge down in black and white, sort out which item is the most pressing. No income? That's pressing. Write out a list of every possible way in which you could make money, big and small.

If I had to do it over again, I would forget about nickel-and-diming myself to death when it comes to making money or paying off debts, and focus instead on the big wins because they give you a much better return on your most important asset, your time. Who wants to live a penny-pinching life or make money in increments of $1.75? You can, but boy is it ever painful. Watching every tiny expenditure is a great way to bleed your soul dry. So where you can, enjoy your cup of coffee and concentrate on the big wins.

START WITH SOMETHING SMALL

Still, sometimes all we can do immediately is something small. Fine, do something small. Move forward in any way you can, and do not stop until you reach your goal. Write down that goal and plaster it everywhere—on your bathroom mirror, beside your bed, next to your desk, in your wallet, on your fridge, in your car, and anywhere else that you can think of. Keep reminding yourself of the two most important things: why you're doing it and what you're accomplishing.

Don't underestimate the power of your creativity, even if you're convinced you don't have a creative bone in your body. The fact is we are all tremendously resourceful when we choose to be. It sounds simplistic, but it works.

I once tutored someone for a statistics course who kept insisting she was terrible at stats and would never pass the course. I tried to encourage her and cajole her into changing her perspective until I finally became frustrated and blurted out in exasperation, "Well as long as you keep maintaining that you're lousy at stats, you will remain lousy at stats. You won't stand a chance until you open up your mind to the possibility of learning statistics."

> "Whether you think you can,
> or think you can't, you're right."
>
> — HENRY FORD

Remember that if you're tackling a big problem, you have to be open to finding a solution before one can be found. And don't expect all of the answers to come at once. As you move forward, options and solutions will present themselves to you. As you work on one solution, you may think of another clever way of paying off your debt. Your actions may open doors of opportunity you'd never thought of. Debt is a solvable problem.

As Malcolm would say, "Two words for you: remain open." I would add to that two more words: trust yourself.

WE'RE OK, BUT AM I OK?

A man is not a financial plan.

— KIM KIYOSAKI

During my interviews with widows and divorcees, I asked them if they had seen the traumatic turn of events coming. Were there any signs? Did they have any suspicions? Did they have an inkling from the outset of the relationship?

> **In every single case, the divorce or the loss**
> **came as a complete surprise.**

To phrase it another way, not one of the women with whom I spoke expected to be on her own before old age, yet that's exactly what happened. Their ages at the time of loss ranged from their mid-twenties to their late-forties. These aren't old women, and now they're facing their futures as solo parents with financial challenges.

The real problem is our disbelief. We think we will never become one of the statistics. Our marriage is strong, we're doing well financially, we're healthy; it's all good. So here's my question: if everyone is doing so well, where do all of the divorces and the deaths come from?

Whenever I do a speaking engagement on this topic, I find virtually no women who are prepared to admit that their marriage, or their partner's health, is in trouble. It's a curious thing. Apparently most of the women I speak to believe they're doing well, yet nearly 50% of the population is either divorced or widowed.

It's challenging enough to consider the risks if you're in a two-income household, but what if you're a stay-at-home mom with no independent income of your own? If your marriage ends, you're stuck financially. What do you do?

When I first began my blog in 2012, I received the following email from a woman in Toronto whom we'll call Peggy:

"I don't have a good 'wish I had known' story, but I thought I might share two recurrent conversations I seem to be having with friends. The first is about what to do about going back to work (or not) when your youngest is in full-day school. For some friends, they had just finished PhDs or had jobs they didn't like so there is no career to which to return. In other cases, they feel a bit stuck because in the time that has passed since they started staying home, their entire family ecosystem has evolved so mom does all the house stuff, including getting kids to activities. So her possible return to work has logistical, social, and emotional impacts in addition to the basic and large impact of needing extra help. Perhaps there is a 'I wish I had known' discussion in there?

The other conversation many of us keep having is about our desire for a 'wife,' a 'secretary,' or a rent-a-grandparent. I'm not sure what the 'I wish I had known' story is in there, but that topic sure resonates with forty-ish moms in my group of friends."

The situations Peggy describes above are central to some of the recommendations I make in this book. In my case, I gave up a PhD to help my late husband Malcolm run the business he had started just one year before.

It concerns me when I see women set themselves up to be dependent on their partner's income while managing mostly unpaid family work. I get it. I'm a mom, and I do most of the running around and planning and so on for our family. I see how the dependence on mom for structural support develops and how difficult it is to re-balance. But my question to all moms is this: if your husband disappeared tomorrow morning, what position would you be in? Let's ask the same questions we asked earlier:

⬧ Where would the money to live on come from? Would there be enough?

⬧ Would it cover your current lifestyle: house, kids' activities, and so on?

⬧ If you have no job to go back to, what will you do? What are your options?

⬧ If your husband died, would you have enough insurance money to cover all of your debts and tide you over while you reinvent yourself? If you're divorcing, there is no insurance to help out.

⬧ Would you have enough money to hire the help you would doubtless need to take care of the unpaid work you used to do?

⬧ Would you have enough to help out with your kids' education?

Going back to work or discovering another career might cause short-term pain, but the pain may be worth it in some circumstances. Each family's situation is unique so there is no single answer for everyone. Asking "what if" simply serves as a powerful tool to look beyond the assumptions we've made about our lives. Few widows expect to become widows. Every divorcee I've known went into her marriage thinking it would last forever.

My goal is to encourage women to ask uncomfortable questions and to set up some buffers right now while they have the time and emotional resources to do it. If your reply is that you're insanely busy at the moment, just try handling your current workload while dealing with death or divorce and the myriad of emotions that go along with it. We never know just how easy we had it until somebody pulls the rug out from under us.

If your response is that you can't afford to rebalance the situation at home, then you are in an even more precarious position. Perhaps consider putting your creativity to work and ask, "How could I afford to have someone else do more of the work at home?" or "How can I protect myself financially? What would it take?" Creativity works its magic once we give it time and space.

If you really enjoy being at home and can't stomach the thought of leaving, then explore some work-at-home options. If you disliked your previous work, as I did, then take the opportunity to explore what brings you joy. Find a way to get paid to do the work you love.

If you don't know what your passions are, then you might find it helpful to read *The Passion Test* by Janet Bray Attwood and Chris Attwood. Their book helped me refocus my energies on the things that really matter to me. The book you are currently reading is the result of a long process of identifying my passions.

I recently interviewed Gail Vaz-Oxlade, a well-known writer and speaker on personal finances, and she had a different take on the issue of stay-at-home moms. Here are her suggestions:

◈ If you are a stay-at-home mom, you do not have zero income—you have a shared income. You and your spouse have decided the best use of your time is to stay at home, therefore, his income becomes a shared income to which you have equal rights.

◈ With that shared income, you pay for all of the essentials, including savings and debt repayment. Whatever is left is then divvied up 50/50.

◈ You and your spouse then choose what you wish to spend your 50% of discretionary cash on. If you're hooked on manicures and pedicures, it comes out of your spending cash. If he wants to indulge in an expensive hobby like high-end bikes, drinking beer, or playing golf with his buddies every weekend, it comes out of his fun money.

◈ You don't get a say on how your spouse spends his fun money, nor does he get to tell you what to do with yours.

◈ If one spouse brings in a much larger salary than the other, the expenditures are attributed in proportion to the income. That is, if you bring in 65% of the household income, then you are responsible for 65% of the expenditures and so on.

Hers is an interesting approach which neatly addresses the issue of the stay-at-home parent. It also makes each spouse responsible for their own discretionary spending.

I'm a big fan of including debt and savings in the budget essentials instead of assigning them to discretionary spending. Where the above approach becomes complicated and potentially less effective, though, is in two key areas.

First, what if both people participate in expensive, shared activities, but to different extents? For example, what if both spouses like to drink expensive wines but one partner outdrinks the other by a large margin. Do you really start to count who drinks how much? "Listen, you had two-thirds of the bottle of wine so you need to pay more." I can't see how that would end well or be practical to implement.

The second, and potentially larger, consideration is that of possible negative outcomes: what would happen in the event of your spouse's death or a divorce? If you're a stay-at-home parent and you implement Gail's system, then you're fine as long as a) your marriage remains intact; b) you invest in retirement vehicles equally; and c) his income remains stable. If he dies or you get divorced, then you may be in trouble even if he faithfully pays for child support and alimony.

While Gail's approach may provide a feasible solution for today's cash, it doesn't address the "what if" scenario that I've raised throughout this book. It also doesn't address the issue of stay-at-home moms who have no marketable employment skills in the event of that loss.

In the end, what I have learned is that everything we do in life involves a choice. Sadly, most of our choices are made unconsciously. We find ourselves moving along a path without really knowing how we ended up there. Whether we like it or not, that's still a choice. What I'm hoping you'll do is explore some of those choices and ask "Is this the best choice for me and my family? Am I happy and protected?"

Regarding Peggy's second conversation with her friends, I have joked that my next husband will be a wife.

14

SUDDEN DEATH

TERESA

Teresa was first married at a young age and had four children in fairly quick succession. When her marriage fell apart, she was left with little money and four young kids to raise on her own. She worked hard for a few years and managed to keep things together, but it was a real struggle. Then she met her second husband, Kevin. He was charming, confident, and by all outward appearances financially successful as a financial planner with a thriving business. The relationship blossomed quickly and they soon moved in together. Four years later, they were married.

One morning eighteen months after their wedding, Teresa was upstairs in her home when she heard her son cry out from the kitchen. She went racing down to find Kevin on the floor by the breakfast table, unconscious and breathing with great difficulty. He died minutes later, having had a massive heart attack. He was in his forties.

Teresa's world began to unravel at that moment. While trying to deal with the shock and grief of Kevin's sudden death, she began the long process of sorting out his financial affairs. The first of many shocks came when she remembered he did not have a will. She had attempted to speak to him about it on several occasions but he refused to discuss it. **Now she was angry with herself for not pressing the issue of writing a will. That was her first lesson.**

The next lesson was even more difficult: he had virtually no savings and was awash in debt. They had always maintained separate bank accounts so she never really knew any of his financial details. He took care of most of the household costs, including paying $2,600 in rent which, as it turns out, they could not afford. After stripping most of his savings to pay for other debt, he had used borrowed funds from a line of credit to pay for their wedding and honeymoon. All that time he had led Teresa to believe he was using his own money to pay for everything. There was never any mention of debt or difficulties. In the end, his estate was declared insolvent, which means there was not enough cash to cover the debts, and Teresa was left with thousands of dollars in legal bills.

Since Kevin was self-employed, there was no pension or income from his business. When Teresa did a bit more digging, she discovered Kevin earned a fraction of what she was led to believe, and his income was dwindling because of difficulties at work. The amount he contributed to their household was not in fact coming from his work; it was mostly coming from borrowed funds.

But there's insurance right? Yes, however it was inadequate. While it did help Teresa clear off some of her existing debt, she was nonetheless left in a precarious situation. The funeral alone cost $10,000. Sadly all widows discover dying is an expensive business.

The most pressing issue, though was that Teresa was tied into a lease for a house she could not afford. When she spoke with the landlord, he was unsympathetic. She eventually extricated herself from the lease after a battle, but then she had to move her family out of their beloved neighborhood. Another trauma.

Thankfully, Teresa has a very supportive family and a job that allowed her to take several months off work to deal with the issues and to grieve. She is now in a much better place financially, but it has been difficult for her and her children. She has had to work through feelings of anger, betrayal, shock, and isolation. When I asked her if she had advice for women, her response was an emphatic yes!

Take it from Teresa:

◈ Insist on full financial disclosure. Know the balances and details of every account, every investment, and every debt. Be sure to have a list of his passwords as well.

◈ Do not depend on your spouse for your standard of living. If they leave or die, can you pay for everything yourself? If not, then make a plan.

◈ Always have emergency funds available in your own name, whether in the form of savings or a line of credit.

◈ Ensure you have a valid will with all wishes outlined in detail.

◈ Be honest with yourself when you enter a serious relationship. Discuss your values and expectations regarding finances. If you are not on the same page, you may want to ask why and ensure you have your own resources.

BARBARA

Some things in life are supposed to be guaranteed. If you take care of your body, you expect to be healthy. When you do all the right things and make the right choices, you reasonably expect to live a long, healthy life. But shortly after her thirtieth birthday, Barbara discovered that in fact, life offers no such guarantees.

Barbara met her husband, Edward, in her early twenties. He was the picture of health: a former professional athlete who exercised regularly, never drank or smoked, and always made wise food choices. From the beginning they had a strong connection. They dated for a couple of years, were engaged for a few more, and then were married. At the start of their engagement they bought a house together. Barbara joked that they would have twins, a boy and a girl, to complete their family and get it all done at once.

Edward had three boys from a previous marriage. When he married Barbara, the kids came to live with them full time since the children's mother had moved away to pursue her own interests. Barbara had already spent quite a bit of time with them as Edward had shared custody, and the boys came to live with them every other week. She loved them as though they were her own.

Two years after marrying, life couldn't be better for Barbara and Edward. To their delight, they had just discovered they were expecting twins! What a lovely, funny twist given Barbara's earlier joke. Then one day after work, Edward went into the kitchen with one of the boys to work on dinner while Barbara went to change. Without any warning he collapsed. Within seconds he was dead. Barbara later found out he'd had heart disease that had gone undetected during a full physical exam just six months earlier. A few days before, Edward had felt a bit dizzy while removing his shoes at the end of the day, but it was not particularly noteworthy so he didn't worry about it. That was the only symptom he ever had.

THEY HAD NEVER TALKED ABOUT THIS TYPE OF SITUATION BECAUSE NEITHER OF THEM THOUGHT IT WOULD EVER HAPPEN TO THEM.

Like so many women who are suddenly widowed, Barbara recalled Edward did not have a will. What was to happen with his children? They had never talked about this type of situation because neither of them thought it would ever happen to them.

While Barbara loved the children, all teenagers by this time, she had a difficult relationship with Edward's ex-wife. His ex had mostly disappeared from the children's lives, yet suddenly she wanted the kids to go live with her on a part-time basis. She called Barbara to ask if they could resume the one-week-on, one-week-off arrangement. Barbara told the kids her home was their home, and they chose to stay with her. After a few months she encouraged the kids to re-establish a relationship with their mother, which they reluctantly did. They began with short visits, but it didn't last long. One of the kids went to live with relatives and the other two stayed with Barbara.

Then there was the issue of finances. Since Barbara and Edward each had salaried jobs with benefits and pensions, they were doing quite well. He had a reasonable life insurance policy through his work and had told Barbara he wanted it split four ways between her and the kids. Barbara honored that request, but it didn't leave her with much money, certainly not enough to pay off the mortgage and to cover their debts. She had her own insurance policy for him, which helped to pay off those liabilities, but it didn't leave her with any extra money to live on or to set aside for her unborn twins.

Barbara regrets that they didn't take more time to consider their insurance needs. Yes, you have to pay off the mortgage and the debts, but what about setting money aside for the kids? Or having money to live on for a while to ease the stress while you grieve? There is enough going on emotionally after such a loss without having to worry about money on top of it all. Grieving is long, hard work.

Thankfully, Barbara received disability pay while she took time off to deal with multiple challenges: the trauma of losing her husband, the stress of figuring out what to do with his children, and the physical demands of a pregnancy, with twins no less.

Here are Barbara's suggestions for other women:

⬦ Ensure you have an up-to-date will with *all* of the details mapped out, particularly regarding children and money.

⬦ If you get into a relationship with someone who already has children, you must talk about what to do with the kids in the event of a tragedy. Do not assume it won't happen. Ensure that the ex-spouse is in agreement. If she isn't, there will be more stress and difficulty. Once there is a plan to which everyone can agree, put it in writing in the will.

⬦ Plan your life insurance carefully to ensure security beyond paying off immediate liabilities.

DEB

(Deb has requested I avoid specific details that could identify her, as the matter is going before the court. Therefore, the vagueness regarding the medical details in this case is intentional.)

Deb's husband Matthew was a healthy guy in his forties. When he complained about a bit of pain in his upper body, Deb didn't think too much about it. Matt didn't either but went to see a medical practitioner all the same. The practitioner couldn't really find anything and thought it might be an infection. He gave Matt some Tylenol 3s and sent him home. Then Matt developed headaches that came and went. He returned to the specialist, who again couldn't find anything. More painkillers were prescribed.

Shortly afterwards, Matt developed an excruciating headache. This time he went to the emergency department of the local hospital. Matt told the doctor his story and was sent home with morphine.

The situation deteriorated and Matt began vomiting. Deb quickly called the emergency ward and spoke to the doctor. She was told morphine can take a while to work and that it should kick in soon. When it was clear the morphine was having no effect, a relative drove Matt back to emergency, where he was sent home after being given some anaesthetic.

Deb knew something was terribly wrong when Matt began to babble and hallucinate. She called the pharmacist to ask if this behavior could be due to an overdose of morphine. She was told the symptoms did not indicate an overdose.

Her next call was to 911 because Matt was in cardiac arrest. He was pronounced dead a short while later.

The coroner later discovered that Matt had an undetected medical issue. Ironically, statistics show it is extremely rare to die from this type of issue.

It is hard to imagine the shock and the feelings that Deb experienced after losing her husband in this way. How was it possible that her healthy, forty-four-year-old husband was dead so suddenly and so unexpectedly? Her grief was overwhelming.

Deb told me, **"The most difficult part was the number of major decisions that need to be made right away when you are still in shock and you can barely function."**

On top of the emotional trauma, Deb soon faced other, practical challenges. Thankfully Matt had a will and insurance, so that bit was taken care of. However, Matt was also the one to take care of most of the bill payments and financial decisions. Deb now had to sort all of that out on her own.

Deb is educated, smart, professional, and capable. Still, it was overwhelming and not because finances were beyond her abilities, but because she faced all of it so suddenly, on her own, at a time when her mental resources were fully taxed.

For example, one of the challenges was the need to refinance her mortgage. Deb remembers sitting in the bank hearing her account manager talk to her about refinance details and all she could think was, "Can I afford the house on my own? Do I still have a roof over my head?"

In the early days of grieving, it is nearly impossible to process information of any kind, let alone mortgage details. Deb was lucky to have a relative present at that meeting. He worked through the details with her afterwards as she struggled to make sense of everything.

At one point, the banker asked if Deb had a credit card. Yes, absolutely. She pulled the card out of her wallet and handed it to the banker who then promptly cut it up because it was a spousal card. The credit card was in Matt's name. Deb's card was an additional card, which means the account wasn't in her name. Interestingly, Matt's card didn't get cut up, just Deb's. She would have to re-apply for a card of her own.

It ended up taking several weeks for Deb to receive her new credit card. As she wryly notes, if she had been a student, companies would likely have thrown cards at her. But as a mature woman establishing her own credit, it took weeks. That can cause some difficulties if you have automatic payments set up through your cards or if you're used to paying for regular purchases like gas and groceries with credit cards. Of course it's doable without them, but it is a pain, especially when you're grieving.

It has only been a couple of years since Matt's death, but Deb is doing amazingly well as she rebuilds her life and finds a new path without him. She has every reason to be bitter and angry, and yet she is warm, open, and determined to remain focused on the positive.

Deb has learned many lessons throughout this whole experience. Here is what she wishes to pass on to all women:

◈ Have a will. When you're young you never expect death to knock at your door, but it does. Ensure that both you and your partner have an up-to-date will.

⟡ Participate in paying the bills. It's important to know what's going on in your family's finances. It is so stressful and difficult to have to figure it out on your own afterwards. Do it right from the beginning and get involved.

⟡ Have your name on all of the assets! This is so important. If your name is on the house, the car, and everything else you own, it's simple to transfer the asset to your name in case of your spouse's death.

⟡ Have your own credit card, not a spousal card. You need to establish your own credit and have a card that you can keep in the event of your spouse's death.

⟡ Plan out guardianship for your children. Pick somebody, or the state will pick for you. Have a plan in place. Your children are too important to let fear paralyze you into inaction.

15

THE DIFFERENCE
PREPARATION MAKES

There is no time on the clock or calendar
called "later." Later never happens.

— KATE BEEDERS

The following are two stories that provide an excellent example of contrasting outcomes. In both cases there was a sudden death, yet the consequences for the families left behind couldn't have been more different. They all hinged on preparation, one of the major points we'll address in the coming chapters. How ready are you to deal with a traumatic event such as loss, divorce, illness, or job loss?

When reading the advice of women I've interviewed, it is easy to nod along. We can agree we should look into some things immediately, but then forget about them entirely. We all mean to get to our list of important to-do items but, well, you know, we're so busy and time just goes flying by.

These two stories illustrate the better financial outcome and the worst financial outcome after a death, and why it's worth taking the time to put some key, protective documents in place.

CONSIDER CASE #1:

Mom was an eighty-year-old woman who had never experienced much illness despite a life of virtual inactivity. She was certainly overweight, but beyond that she did not appear to have any significant health issues. Her two adult children, a daughter and a son in their thirties and forties, respectively, lived with her and depended on her for survival as they were both unemployed. Mom never worked outside the home, so when her husband Len died, she lived off his pension.

Len's will ensured the estate passed on to his wife without issue. Mom, on the other hand, did not have a will. She understood its importance, but when the kids pressed her about it she made excuses: too expensive, not the right time, not necessary at the moment, she'll get around to it in good time.

One morning Mom didn't get out of bed. She had died of a heart attack in her sleep. Now the kids were in a real bind. The only money available—a relatively modest amount—was in Mom's various bank accounts, and those would be frozen until her estate was processed through probate to determine the heirs. There was no mortgage on the house, but taxes and utilities needed to be paid, not to mention their need for food. There was also car insurance for a vehicle that was necessary given the location of the house. Also, pension payments ended the day Mom died.

When I spoke with the children, the process of probate had just begun and, in the best-case scenario, assuming the court process went reasonably smoothly and doesn't suffer delays, the son and daughter could expect the matter to take six to eight weeks to be resolved. Again, that was the best possible outcome.

The daughter was in the hospital with a terminal illness. The son would have difficulty finding employment given he had been out of the work force for more than a decade. The family house, in which the son lived, was in terrible physical condition and would require a substantial investment in order to make it sale-ready.

Prior to that consideration, there was the issue of accumulated clutter from a lifetime of hoarding. The house couldn't be emptied because there was no money for something as simple as a dumpster.

The most likely outcome would be having to eventually sell the house as-is for a price significantly below market, if he's lucky. Its condition would make finding a buyer difficult. Even if he were to sell the place at a greatly reduced price, which is an unlikely event, he wouldn't end up with much given that house values in that area are already quite modest.

Sadly, the grim situation outlined above could largely have been avoided with a simple will.

Now let's take a look at another scenario.

CASE #2: ANN'S STORY

Ann and Tim were a successful, healthy, middle-aged couple with two adult children. Years ago they had bought an IT company and grew it into a reasonably large enterprise with several employees. The growth was due to a couple key factors: Tim's technical and marketing savvy, and Ann's careful financial planning.

For fifteen years they had talked about taking a holiday alone yet somehow had never quite managed it. Work was busy, they had a large house to maintain, and then there were the kids' activities. There just never seemed to be enough time to travel.

Finally, in November of 2007, they took the plunge. The kids had just moved out and they decided it was time to treat themselves. Off they went to Barbados.

The rented condo was gorgeous and so was the weather. For the first couple of days, they played in the surf and relaxed by the ocean. Tim got battered about by the waves, but it didn't seem to matter; he loved the water so much he couldn't get enough of it. By the third day though, he was complaining of a bruised rib and decided it would be prudent to take it easy for a while. They both relaxed by the ocean that day until it was time to get ready for a cocktail party hosted by the complex's manager.

Around 4 pm, Ann went back up to the condo to have a shower. She was just getting out when she heard someone banging on the door. It was the manager.

"Come to the beach right now. Something's happened to your husband. I think he's dead."

The condo complex was located at the top of a hill adjacent to the beach. There were what appeared to be a thousand steps to get down. As Ann descended, she saw one lawn chair on the beach with a large group of people standing around it. All other chairs had been removed. Tim was seated on the chair, eyes open, looking out at the ocean, but his chest wasn't moving. He was dead.

Ann was stunned. She reached out for his hand, closed his eyes and sat down next to him, unable to say or think anything at all. The condo staff eventually cleared all of the people away. The next thing Ann knew, men in black shirts showed up and took control. Ann later learned that the black-shirted men were all ex-military Canadians working as security staff for a wealthy Canadian, Mr. H, who lived in the area. Word of a death on the beach had gotten out and they came to help.

For the next several hours, the security men called the police and the coroner, and eventually talked Ann into going back up to the condo to call family members.

The whole experience was unreal—Ann couldn't make any sense of it. Tim was the healthiest guy she knew. How could this happen? She knew perfectly well that if she thought about it too much she would be overwhelmed with emotion, so she buried all of her feelings and focused instead on the tasks in front of her. She needed to track down her son and daughter, and her in-laws. There were business calls to be made in addition to figuring out how to get Tim's body back to Canada. She also had to call her insurance representative. The details were overwhelming.

A significant stumbling block soon presented itself. The funeral home and insurance company were arguing over who would pay. The funeral home required payment before they would proceed, and they refused to accept anything other than cash. Cash was the only thing Ann didn't have. Who travels with a lot of cash these days? She had checks and credit cards, none of which were acceptable to the funeral home. Mr. H, who had been calling and visiting her daily, showed up to the condo with a blank check in hand. "Use whatever you need to get things done. We'll work it out later."

His generosity didn't end there. He gave Ann a cell phone and assigned some of his security staff directly to her. They were to take her wherever she needed to go. When her daughter Margaret arrived, Mr. H's wife not only picked her up at the airport, she also showed up with a bag of clothes, shoes, and jewelry. She had heard that Margaret's luggage had not made it to the island. The support that Mr. H and his family provided was outstanding.

After multiple challenges, including experiencing the island's first-ever earthquake, Ann finally made it home. Tim's brother followed with Tim's remains a few days later. At long last they were back in Canada.

Money was not an issue for Ann as she and Tim had been wise from the very beginning. He had a will, they had a generous insurance policy, and Tim also had insurance at work. In short, Ann was financially set and, since she ran the company, she knew exactly where everything was and what she had to do. There were no shocking discoveries or frantic searches for key documents. Everything was where it needed to be and the financial supports were in place.

It was clear to Ann she could not continue to run the company without Tim, nor could she simply abandon it. Since several employees depended on the business for their livelihood, something had to be done. During the year that followed Tim's death, Ann split the company into its component parts and sold each one to people who would continue to grow it.

The biggest challenge Ann faced, beyond the shock and emotional trauma of losing her husband so suddenly, was determining what she wanted to do with her life. She has since explored a couple of different paths and is continuing to seek out her passions.

The reason that Ann has the freedom to redefine her future at her own pace is simply because she made smart choices along the way. When I explored the source of her financial wisdom, Ann pointed to her parents' influence. As a young child, she was included in trips to the bank and conversations about budgets. She learned to look and plan ahead, and to honor cash flow above all else. The lessons began at an early age and continued throughout her time at home.

Today, Ann has the following advice for women:

⊕ *Read books on finance and ensure that you are taken care of. Don't stick your head in the sand and above all, don't assume that something won't happen to you. Protect yourself now. Right now.*

If you've been thinking you really need to create or revise a will and buy sufficient insurance but you haven't had the time, or if you're putting it off because you think it's too expensive, just ask yourself: what would Doris write about my situation if I became a case study tomorrow?

The point of the case studies mentioned in this chapter is to illustrate that a bit of planning makes all the difference when tragedy strikes. Since we often don't see tragedy coming, the time to get your financial house in order is right now.

16

ON MEN AND TOOLS

I learned to always take on things I'd never done
before. Growth and comfort do not coexist.

— Virginia Rometty

 pop quiz for women:

① What are the names of screw drivers that have a square-shaped
tip and a star-shaped tip, respectively?
   A. Masters and Johnson
   B. Calvin and Hobbes
   C. Robertson and Phillips
   D. Rodgers and Hammerstein

② How do you change the direction of rotation on a drill?
   A. Who cares?
   B. You can't. It spins only one way.

C. By switching a lever typically located on or near the bottom of the handle.

D. By cursing at it.

③ Why do screw drivers have differently colored handles?
   A. To match the furniture.
   B. To match the season.
   C. Each color represents a different size.
   D. Each color is used for a different job.

④ In renovations, mudding refers to what?
   A. The mess left behind by careless contractors.
   B. A process used in plumbing.
   C. The use of a compound to cover seams after drywall is installed.
   D. A painting technique.

You're probably wondering why on earth I am talking about tools and renovations in a book about sharing lessons with women. I'll get to that.

First, how comfortable are you with maintaining your house and dealing with machines or systems that break down in your world? Perhaps you have come to a good place after many trials and learning experiences, or perhaps you've learned the hard way, as I did. What we all know is that everything breaks down eventually and houses need a great deal of maintenance.

So why are women, as a whole, so unprepared for it all?

These days I'm in a good place when it comes to repairing things but it's been a long road to get here. Ironically, after everything I've been through, I'm now the handy one in my marriage. Mark is someone for whom the idea of manual labor involves a corkscrew and a wine glass, and whose idea of home repairs involves the use of a telephone and a credit card. I see the genius in his approach, but I'm nonetheless glad I was forced to figure it out.

When I met Mark, three things struck me: his library (large and varied), his red wine collection (impressive), and his tool box (not so much). The latter inspired a Crocodile Dundee moment: "That's not a tool box, that's a jewelry box. *This* is a tool box." When we moved in together, we kept mine and my large collection of tools.

The tool collection came courtesy of Malcolm, who was a gifted tool user and buyer. There was nothing he couldn't create or a tool sale he could resist. As a result I had, and eventually learned to use, a vast collection of tools, powered and otherwise. When Malcolm became too ill to work, his father, Ron, handed me a drill, showed me how to use it, and put me to work installing floors and drywall in the industrial space that we were building. After several years of hanging out with Ron, I could build or repair pretty much anything thanks to his tutelage. From 1996 to 1998 I learned to do a lot of things I never imagined likely for me, but the hardest part began after Malcolm's death.

THE UNEXPECTED HAPPENS

The first Christmas after Malcolm's death, the universe decided to test my survival skills. Christmas can be challenging at the best of times, but when you're immersed in a world of grief, it's impossible. As soon as the last of the Christmas sales was over, I retreated to my country house, locked the door, and ignored the world.

I'm not sure when I realized my house felt cold. My first reaction was to turn up the heat, to no effect. Our house had a geothermal system so there was never a sound of the furnace starting; it was more like a constant movement of air. The problem was that the air had stopped moving and there was certainly no heat. I wasn't immediately concerned, as this had happened before. I turned the system off, waited a bit, and then turned it on again, thinking it would reset itself as it had in the past. Still nothing. That's when I started to panic.

The furnace was located in a crawl space underneath the stairs in the basement. My first thought was to go look at the thing, an idea quickly overridden by an awareness that I didn't know the first thing about heating systems, geothermal or otherwise, so what would looking at it accomplish? I searched everywhere for the manual the previous owners had left behind. I found a phone number to call for servicing. Perfect. Except they were closed for the holidays and would only reopen again in several days. The recording recommended I call a local company for assistance. Which local company? I called a few, but no one had a clue about geothermal systems. I was told to call the manufacturer. Great.

Just as panic was starting to rise in my throat, I closed my eyes and talked to Malcolm: "What am I supposed to do now? It's really cold outside and I have no heat."

I figured I may as well have a look at the thing, hoping some action was better than none. I crawled into the space next to the furnace, brushing away cobwebs as I looked for buttons. What I found was an array of flashing lights and a few buttons. What to do? Once again, I closed my eyes and asked Malcolm for help. I didn't hear anything, nor did I have an epiphany about how geothermal systems work, but I did feel a sense of calm come over me, and I began to push buttons. Eventually something worked and the unit began to hum once again.

A few days later I spoke to a technician and got him to write out instructions in case this happened again. "But you figured it out; you don't need my help," he said. No, I got lucky. I have no idea what I did to make the machine work. That won't help me in the future.

INTERNATIONAL SYMBOLS

A few weeks later a massive amount of snow fell, so much so that I couldn't get my car out of the garage. We had a 2.2-acre property with a massive driveway. There was no way I could shovel the whole thing in a reasonable amount of time. I was forced to use the snow blower, something I had never done before. Malcolm had bought it the moment we moved to the country property, telling me it would be essential.

"I love this thing," he'd said the first time he'd used it, "It's so easy to use and look at the amount of snow I can move in minutes with it!"

Now, it was my turn to figure out how to use it. Okay, no problem. I've used a riding lawn mower on the farm where I was raised. I drove motorcycles as a kid. How hard can it be to use a snow blower? I had the key and knew the basics.

Fifteen minutes later I still hadn't got the thing started. There was no point in searching for an instruction manual because Malcolm had never seen the need for such a thing. He was one of those people who seem to have an innate understanding of how everything works; there wasn't a single machine he couldn't pull apart and put together again.

I finally broke down and called Ron. Ron was the original Mr. Fix It. He was also an erudite Scot with no tolerance for stupidity.

"Doris, can't you tell from the symbols on the front? They're called international symbols for a reason. They're supposed to be obvious."

"Ron, these symbols were apparently designed by a fine art student in Mali who has never seen snow. You may as well ask a kindergarten child to explain how to get the thing started—she'd probably do a better job. Maybe one of them is Japanese for "Call your father-in-law in case of problems." Yes, I put the key in and turned it on. Yes, I've done that too. And that. No, it still doesn't start. Yes, I'd like to choke the thing. Wait, what do you mean by choke? Oh. No, haven't done that. How do you do that again?"

With cell phone in hand, wearing Malcolm's size 10 boots on my size 8 feet because I didn't own any tall enough to keep the snow out, I finally got the beast started. As soon as I freed my car from its snowy prison, I drove to the store, got a copy of the manual, and read it cover to cover.

GETTING RIPPED OFF

A few months later I had contractors in to remove a door and install a window in its place. Malcolm and I had meant to do that from the very beginning, but with his illness taking over, we hadn't managed it.

The day that the contractors finally came to get the job done something didn't seem right. They were awfully quick about their business and the guys never looked me in the eye. I saw the window go in but wasn't around to see the drywall go up around it. When the job was done they left in a big hurry, saying the boss would bill me for the work.

Something bothered me about the whole thing. As I thought about it, I realized I hadn't seen them bring any insulation into the house. I started tapping on the wall around the window and what I got was a hollow sound. One foot away, my taps yielded the expected dull sound of an insulated wall. I ran down to the tool chest and pulled out a long-handled screw driver. Then, in a moment inspired by a horror movie, I drove it into the drywall above the window. It went right through without any resistance beyond the drywall. I did the same all around the window. I eventually removed a good chunk of the newly-installed drywall to reveal that the contractors had installed a window with no insulation around it. There was one foot of empty space around all sides of my north-east facing window.

The next day I called the owner of the company and asked if he was sure the job had been done properly. He had not been out to inspect it, but yes, indeed, he was certain his contractors had done a bang-up job with their usual professionalism. I invited him to drop by my house to have a look at the work before I paid him. He said it wasn't necessary. I insisted. In the end, I got a hefty discount and a sheepish apology with assurances that kind of thing had never happened before. I also watched the contractors like a hawk as they did the job a second time.

The reality is that single women get taken advantage of by service providers, particularly when it comes to areas traditionally the domain of men. Here, then, is my suggestion to an entrepreneurial Mr. Fix It out there: Start a business called Replacement Husband Contracting Services. Your motto can be "Honest, reliable service with no strings attached and nothing to clean up for a change." I would have hired such a "Replacement Husband" in a heartbeat that Christmas, and I bet a lot of single women would do the same today.

THE REALITY IS THAT SINGLE WOMEN GET TAKEN ADVANTAGE OF BY SERVICE PROVIDERS, PARTICULARLY WHEN IT COMES TO AREAS TRADITIONALLY THE DOMAIN OF MEN.

Women need honest people they can turn to when the various machines and systems in their lives fail. It's a huge and probably profitable niche. If you start such a business, let me know; I will gladly promote you.

Most of us women never spend any time learning how to use basic tools and figuring out how some common items work. We should. Yes, our fathers should teach us everything they know. My brother knew how to change the oil in a car as a teenager, yet I was never taught. That is, not until after Malcolm's death, when I sought out a program for women offered through a local car dealership (brilliant idea, by the way).

Even if our fathers teach us nothing at all, it is still our responsibility to learn some of the basics. Why? Because it helps us to be better prepared and to feel more confident in the face of challenges.

KNOWLEDGE BREEDS CONFIDENCE

You may decide you never want to swing a hammer or hold a drill and that's okay, but it is nonetheless valuable to understand the basics so you can evaluate a potential contractor. Knowledge breeds confidence and choice. It also yields respect from contractors. When you know something about repairs, it changes the whole dynamic when speaking with tradesmen. And let's face it, they're pretty much all men.

I cannot emphasize enough the power of choice. Isn't that ideally what we want for ourselves—the freedom to choose our outcomes? That same philosophy applies to repairs. I know how to do a number of renovations, but I now choose not to. I spent enough of my twenties and early thirties putting in floors and walls; I never want to do that again. I'd rather take Mark's approach—write a check and use the time doing something I value more.

Wherever you are on the learning curve, I encourage you to gain more knowledge and to begin the process of demystifying the world of tools and machines. It's really not that complicated once you get past the fear. Ask questions of repair people, and don't be afraid of looking or sounding stupid. People who ask questions get answers, and people who get answers gain knowledge. As you increase your knowledge, you increase your personal power. Think of how profound a lesson that is for your kids. You—and they—are worth the investment of a bit of time.

My final words on this subject, though are addressed to the men in your life. I know this book is aimed at women, but there is one key point to pass on to your partners: teach your daughters what you know, every last bit of it. It's great that you love and support your daughter in her endeavors. Now teach her what you know, and encourage her to learn, particularly if you work in a domain that is traditionally the preserve of men.

If you're a whiz at technology, share that; if you're a sports hound, get her out there with you, and don't go easy on her. Do you do repairs on the house? Have your daughter assist you, and every once in a while let her take a crack at it. Let her mow the lawn and change the oil in the mower. Get her to use the snow blower; have her repair a dent in the wall or diagnose a problem with the vacuum cleaner. Teach her how to do these things safely and well.

Will she love learning this stuff? Maybe not, but who cares? Few people love to do laundry, yet it has to be done. It's just one of those things we have to learn. Repairs and maintenance are not "men's work," just as laundry is not "women's work."

Incidentally, here's the message that I keep repeating to my daughters, one of whom has just entered her teenage years: if a guy doesn't know how to cook or do his own laundry—or worse, isn't willing to—then he is of no interest to you. Move on. You were put on this earth to use your gifts and create the highest, best possible life for yourself. You are not here to fulfill someone else's idea of "girls' work."

There is no such thing as boys' work or girls' work; there is only work that needs to get done. We all share in the responsibility to tackle it.

THE THING ABOUT LUCK

The only good luck many great men ever
had was being born with the ability and
determination to overcome bad luck.

— CHANNING POLLOCK

A friend of mine was recently diagnosed with breast cancer. After the usual procedures, including surgery and various tests, she discovered chemotherapy would not be necessary for her. Before she learned that though, she had made plans with relatives to take her kids for March break so they wouldn't be home to witness her potential struggle with a difficult treatment.

However, with the absence of chemotherapy, she was now free to spend the entire week doing whatever she chose to do which, among other things, included accompanying her husband to another city, where she caught up with friends and enjoyed some alone time.

Someone told her she was very lucky to have that week alone with her husband, which prompted my friend to write a thoughtful post on social media about luck being a complicated lady.

Was my friend really lucky? The reason she had the week alone was a cancer diagnosis and the expectation to start treatment that week. Is that luck? If given the choice, she would have gladly skipped off with her children rather than spend the week without them. The sentiment expressed by her friend was kindly meant, but it did nonetheless elicit a range of emotions and a thought-provoking article.

Ah, luck. What a curious beast.

Remember my story in chapter five about having to stand in a sales booth at a retail show after Malcolm's death? I can't tell you how many people told me I was so lucky to be able to work with my husband and that we must have the best marriage. They meant well, but their words were devastating for me. I realized they didn't know of his death, but it was nonetheless hard to hear how supposedly lucky I was.

When Malcolm died, a few well-intentioned souls, who were likely grasping for something to say to the young widow before them, told me I was lucky not to have any children. At least I didn't have that stress hanging over my head during such a difficult time.

Here's the thing: Malcolm was infertile thanks to the many radiation treatments he received when he was fourteen years old, so I didn't have the option of having children with him. Was that really lucky? At moments I certainly thought it was easier, particularly when I felt I couldn't get out of bed in the morning, but then at other moments I wished we could have had children together, that a part of him could live on in our child; I wished we could have shared that experience together. It would have been nice to have had the choice.

Six months later I joined a support group comprised entirely of people in their thirties and forties. When I shared that comment with the group, the lady sitting next to me said, "Interesting. I was told I'm lucky to have children so I can focus on them instead of just me. They think it will help me to get past my grief more quickly. But I don't want to cry in front of the children, so I bottle it up, and now I feel like I'm going to explode. I'm so busy ensuring the kids' lives are as normal as possible that I don't have the time to grieve. So who's lucky? This doesn't feel like luck to me."

The appearance of luck is often misleading. We may see what we believe to be the hallmark of good fortune without necessarily understanding what led to that point. While someone may get a lucky break—something genuinely the result of luck rather than effort—there is usually much more to the story than meets the eye.

Someone once told me that I'm lucky to be thin. They said, "You clearly have your father's genes." Maybe genetics plays a role, but I suspect the fact that I'm mostly disciplined about what I eat (six days of the week anyway) and that I am consistently physically active have something to do with my shape. Is it really just luck that's at play here? If so, then my genes must have abandoned me during the year I taught in France as a twenty-one-year-old, living on baguettes, red wine, and cheese, and packing on the pounds. I left Canada looking svelte and came back a more well-rounded person. What of my genetics then?

At a party a while ago, another person told me that I'm lucky not to know ill health. They didn't know what I've been through, yet they spoke of luck with great ease. I can tell you, having lost a husband at the age of thirty-two, I am more than a bit focused on optimizing for good health. There's an awful lot of effort, and there are many difficult choices behind the so-called luck. Sure, I'm lucky not to have a genetically linked disease, but it's not all about luck.

When someone insists on saying we're lucky, most of us simply agree with the assertion. "Yes, I'm very lucky," we say, "I'm so grateful for my good fortune." We do it because we don't want to appear rude by disagreeing with them. Besides, it's a lot easier than engaging in a lengthy exposition of all of the contributing factors to that so-called luck. It's also socially awkward to explain that our "good fortune" is the result of a tragedy. Who wants to tackle that with an acquaintance?

Interestingly, we seem to instinctively know not to apply the phrase "that's unlucky" to someone's circumstance. Think back to Barbara's husband, who dropped dead of a heart attack in his thirties despite being a professional athlete with no history or record of heart disease. *That's* unlucky and awful. Or Ann's husband, who died on a beach during their first holiday alone in years. That's unlucky and awful, too.

We would not likely feel comfortable telling these ladies they're unlucky. "You poor thing, you've just lost your husband. You're so unlucky." What?! No way. Telling someone they are unlucky isn't helpful, for starters, and it also seems terribly inadequate as a descriptor; "unlucky" doesn't begin to cover it. So why then do we feel comfortable telling people the opposite, that they're lucky?

WHAT IT ACTUALLY MEANS

The use of phrases like this tell us much more about the person using them than about the recipient. When we tell someone they're lucky, what we really mean is that we wish we had their outcome. By saying, "You're lucky to have a week alone with your husband without the kids," what we probably mean is that *we wish we had a week alone with our spouse, without the kids.*

"You're so lucky to be holidaying down south" translates to "I wish we were holidaying down south."

While these expressions seem harmless, behind every such envious statement lurks a touch of scarcity mentality. It's one thing to think,

WHEN WE TELL SOMEONE THEY'RE LUCKY, WHAT WE REALLY MEAN IS THAT WE WISH WE HAD THEIR OUTCOME.

"Hey, I'd love to do that too," but it's quite another to instead focus on what you don't have. By calling someone lucky, you're pretty much saying you couldn't have what they have because it's entirely based on luck. So the focus remains on what you don't have. They are a have; you are a have-not. Where does that get you?

At moments when you're tempted to tell someone they're lucky, consider instead focusing entirely on the other person and feeling genuinely happy for the positive outcome in their life. If it's something you would like or enjoy, then consider saying, "Good for you!" while at the same time asking yourself how you could have, be, or do the same thing. What would it take? This changes the focus from envy to recognition and inspiration.

Wouldn't you rather inspire creativity and get your brain cells working for your own good rather than dwell on what you lack?

BETRAYAL

CATHY

"I'll see you for lunch. I love you."

With those words, Cathy and Dan parted for what should have been another ordinary work day. That was the last time Cathy saw her husband.

During their twenty-three years together, Cathy and Dan had developed a lovely routine of meeting over lunch after their morning's work. Day in, day out, they would connect. There was nothing unusual about the morning of September 16, 2011. Cathy went off to her work as a college professor, and Dan set out to his photography business after a hug, a kiss, and the usual promise of seeing each other at lunch. There was much to look forward to that weekend as they had planned a get-away with friends.

Their younger daughter Natalie met Cathy at the college after her class and asked if she could join in for lunch. They arrived home to find that Dan was not there, nor had he left a note. Cathy called and texted his phone to determine when he would arrive. Uncharacteristically, he did not reply. Fifteen minutes later, Natalie tried to reach her father. Again there was no response, so they started lunch without him.

Shortly afterwards the doorbell rang. Cathy instantly said to her daughter "That's the police." It was nothing more than a gut feeling, yet somehow she knew she was right.

Two officers asked to come in. They informed Cathy that Dan had died of a heart attack and had been pronounced dead at the scene. The impact of those words caused immense shock. Cathy couldn't quite process it all. While some people become paralyzed by such news, Cathy quickly dove into action, calling family members and her parish priest. In the meantime, Natalie checked Dan's phone, which the police had brought, and saw a text from a woman about coming over in the morning. She didn't recognize the name but assumed it was a client. He was, after all, a successful photographer with a long list of clients.

An hour later, a police psychologist arrived and asked to have a word in private. She explained how Dan had been found naked in bed at another woman's house. Cathy's world began to unravel.

It's one thing to lose your husband so suddenly, but it's another thing entirely to discover after the fact that he had been unfaithful for years. On top of the grief, Cathy now faced the devastation of betrayal. Five weeks after Dan's death, Cathy learned he'd had an affair for eight years with a friend of the woman in whose bed he was found. It had taken considerable sleuthing, but she eventually got the answers she sought. Cathy wrote to the woman who was the last person to see Dan alive, to ask if she could get some answers in order for her family to have some closure. She wanted to know how they had met and how long the affair had been going on. The answers broke her heart.

During a face-to-face meeting, Cathy learned that Dan had an affair with the woman's friend for eight years, meeting two to three times a week the entire time. To add insult to injury, they had met at a strip bar, and Dan had made it clear that he was sleeping with a number of other women. For eight years, he had successfully lived a double life.

The pain kept coming: Cathy discovered that roughly $60,000 of their $185,000 debt load came from expenditures on other women for things such as dinners for two at restaurants to which Cathy had never been. Eight years of enjoying other women's company had added up, and now Cathy was liable for it all.

Was there any life insurance, I asked? No. Several years before his death, Dan had cancelled it without discussing it with Cathy. At the time, they had a small child and a mortgage. Cathy had been livid, but Dan insisted they didn't need it.

They also had other debts. Cathy learned that two weeks before he died, Dan had finally completed six years' worth of tax returns, which resulted in a significant tax bill. That amount had yet to be paid. Then there were calls from collection agencies for a variety of other unpaid invoices. The financial picture was overwhelming, but one thing was clear: Cathy was left with a big mess to clean up.

Cathy knew Dan did not have an unblemished record on the matter of fidelity. Thirteen years prior, Cathy discovered Dan's fling with an old flame. The woman in question, who was a guest in their house at the time of the revelation, told Cathy the affair had started before Dan and Cathy met. She claimed it had continued during their engagement and for the first five years of their marriage. The relationship ended only when the woman became engaged and then married. When confronted with this information, Dan initially denied the accusation. The following morning he told Cathy he had been up all night crying and praying, and finally had to admit he had slept with the woman two weeks previously, but only once since his marriage to Cathy.

The news came as a terrible blow. Cathy turned to her faith for guidance, and after some time, prayer, and consultation with a counselor, decided to forgive Dan, in part to keep the family whole. After all, there were children to consider. Their marriage continued with what Cathy believed to be a renewed commitment, which made the final revelations all the more devastating.

Several weeks after the funeral, Dan's sister and brother admitted to Cathy that Dan's first marriage had failed because he had been unfaithful in the first year. Cathy was Dan's fourth wife. Dan apparently had a great reason for every break up: she wanted children, he wanted to go back to university; they married too young and grew apart, and so on. After his death though, the truth began to surface: infidelity had played a role in at least two of the failed marriages.

The last two years of her marriage had been difficult for Cathy. She and Dan were supposed to retire soon and travel the world, enjoying their freedom and good health before the inevitable effects of old age set in. Then she learned Dan was not the brilliant financial manager he had purported to be. He took care of all of the finances and assured Cathy they were on track to retire as they had hoped. However, to her surprise, she discovered they had $150,000 in debt at that time. She had taken several months off work to deal with ongoing issues with depression, but now she would clearly have to go back to work to help pay the bills. Her dream of retirement and travel had vanished. Three weeks after she resumed her work, Dan died and she was left to pick up the pieces of his betrayal, both emotional and financial.

Cathy has experienced terrible lows yet, despite all the trauma, she has managed to get herself to a much better place emotionally. Her resilience and emotional recovery are remarkable given what she has experienced. She offered the following advice for women:

⬧ No matter how fulfilling your relationship with your significant other, women draw strength from their female friends. Have a circle of friends who are mutually supportive and totally trustworthy. Then be there for each other.

❖ Belong to a community. I don't know what I would have done without the support of my faith community and my parish. Though only four people in this community know of Dan's betrayal, the entire community knows of his death. Their prayers, phone calls, cards, hugs, visits, and listening ears have sustained me through dark hours and days.

❖ Nothing could have prepared and protected me from the shock of Dan's betrayal. However, here are some thoughts about dealing with the aftermath:

○ When your world has totally fallen apart and shifted to a place you never thought could exist, and when you understand the meaning of "heartbroken," sometimes all you can do is feel the pain. Just let yourself be in that space.

○ When you can't imagine going on in life and can't think of a reason to bother, think of an earlier time in your life when you were extremely sad and got through it. Let that time remind you that things will get better eventually, even if it doesn't seem that way at present.

○ When loneliness and emptiness threaten to overwhelm you, reach out to someone you can trust to hold you and care for you until you can begin to care for yourself again.

○ Keep an open spirit. Don't become jaded.

KAREN

Karen's plan was fairly straightforward: Find satisfying work, meet a great guy, have two children, and live a joyful life. During her twenties it seemed she was on the right track, particularly when she met Don. He was good looking, charismatic, and charming. The problem was his indecision about a career path.

Within their first few years together he decided to return to college to further his training. While he focused on his studies, Karen worked and bought a house with her brother. It was a great arrangement: Karen lived on the main floor and her brother had the basement to himself. Don eventually moved in with Karen, along with his daughter from a previous marriage. While he paid some rent, Karen carried the majority of the living costs. This was fine by her as she was supportive of Don's efforts to reinvent himself.

The presence of Don's daughter meant that Karen was suddenly placed in a parenting role, to which she adapted happily and quickly. She had always wanted and loved children, and the addition of a step-daughter in her life gave her the opportunity to play a significant part from the beginning. A short while later, she became pregnant with her own daughter. Life seemed to be moving along nicely.

Then everything changed when Don became ill with a neurological disorder that caused uncontrollable shaking and twisting in his neck, making it impossible for him to function normally. He had been working on a contract that was headed for renewal just prior to his illness, but when his health took a turn for the worse, the contract was not renewed. Don remained unemployed for several months. Since Karen had been working at her new job less than one year prior to having her baby, there was no maternity coverage. They had to subsist on Employment Insurance, which did not amount to a lot of money for a family of four.

Over the next few years, Don's illness caused significant problems. He found and lost four jobs, which left their family in a constant state of financial crisis. Karen's stable employment left her as the main breadwinner.

Eventually, Don seemed to find the right dosage for his medications and his physical condition began to stabilize. He found a new job as a manager at a theatre, and while it required all sorts of strange hours,

Karen was nonetheless supportive. She wanted him to make a success of his job after so many difficulties. Unfortunately however, Don had started drinking to excess, following in the footsteps of his alcoholic mother.

When the mortgage for the house came up for renewal, Karen's brother wanted to sell his share. After some discussion with Don, Karen decided it would be best if they sold the house, paid off her brother, and bought a house of their own. They were in the process of trying to have another baby, so it was a perfect time to set out on their own. She was certain things would work themselves out.

During the process of sorting out the housing issue, Don decided to make an independent film. Karen did her best to talk him out of it. They had enough on their plate—a young child, a house to sell, a house to buy, his drinking habit, not to mention their desire to have another baby sometime soon. It was just not a good time for a new venture. Don insisted it was something he needed to do. If he finished it quickly, he would be able to help care for Karen during the pregnancy, unlike the first time. Again, Karen wanted to be supportive so, despite her reservations, she relented.

Don got to work on filming his movie in the basement of their house—a process which required Karen and the girls to vacate the property—while Karen made all the arrangements to sell the house and find a new one.

The film project didn't live up to Karen's expectations. She had hoped it would make Don happy, however, he was becoming more distant and angry as time went on. He'd attribute it to stress from his job, the impending move, and his movie; there were many reasons at the ready when Karen tried to talk to him about it. Things escalated to the point where he was yelling so loudly at his oldest daughter that the neighbors called the police. Karen insisted he go into counseling for anger management and alcohol abuse, as well as marriage counseling. He agreed, but only after the move.

They moved into their new house at the end of August of that year. On October 6, they had their first session with a marriage counselor. On October 7, they celebrated their fifth wedding anniversary. On October 9, his oldest daughter found him in bed with one of the actors in his film. Don pleaded for forgiveness when Karen arrived at the house. It had been only a momentary thing and would never happen again.

Karen was horrified, but she believed him. She desperately wanted her family to be intact for her daughter's sake. She sent him to his mother's house as she tried to process what had happened. Two days later she received an anonymous message on Facebook from someone on the film set claiming Don had been having an affair for some time. Karen immediately left work and headed to Don's office, where she confronted him with the information. For forty-five minutes he denied the allegations and then eventually broke down. He had been taking his mistress to hotel rooms and using their money to do it. In retrospect, it had seemed strange to Karen that he never had money to pay the bills.

She was shocked. The trauma of her discovery prevented her from working and processing information for some time. She had done so much for this man. How could he have done this to her? It was heartbreaking to think that all of her plans and dreams had come crashing down around her. Shock gave way to anger and sadness. Much bitterness still remains to this day.

The positive side to this story is that Karen was surprised by the support she received from all quarters, both professional and personal. People gave her time, money, and a sympathetic ear.

Perhaps the nicest outcome of all is the support Karen received from her step-daughter. Karen says it best: "She has chosen to continue living with me and her little sister as she completes her high school education, and she is most welcome to do so. She is angry with her father, who also cheated on her mom when they were married. She has very little to do with him. By contrast, she has told me over and over that I have been a good mom to her, and she has propped me up when I felt I couldn't stand. We have been there for each other in a way that is really beautiful, and I am exceedingly proud of the kind, intelligent, beautiful young woman she has become. I feel like I have gained a daughter through this."

When I asked Karen what advice she would pass on to other women, she offered the following:

⬦ Don't overlook how a person was raised or their past behavior. People can talk a good game when they are dating, but they will usually revert to the core values with which they were raised. Don cheated on his first wife. That should have set off a flag. His mother was an alcoholic—again another issue. If there are issues in your partner's past, don't ignore them. Look at the ethical values they bring with them from their past.

⬦ Don was never accountable for anything. There was always a story for everything, always someone else in the wrong, someone else to blame. That kind of behavior should be a warning sign.

⬦ If you have a secret you feel you can't share with anyone, that's a red flag for you. By remaining silent, you will continue to victimize yourself, and by keeping his secrets, you are complicit. You must find someone with whom you can talk. Don't carry the burden yourself.

⬦ You are not alone and you have worth. Always remember that.

NOT-SO-GREAT EXPECTATIONS

Argue for your limitations,
and sure enough they're yours.

— RICHARD BACH

Imagine if Charles Dickens' novel had been called *Not-So-Great Expectations*. Not exactly a blockbuster, is it? Oddly, that sentiment seems to be the title governing so many of our lives.

If you were to write an autobiography today and you had to come up with a title for it, what would it be? Would it be inspiring? Would it speak of talents fully utilized, a life lived to its highest potential?

Are you reaching for what's possible, or are you instead aiming for what you think is possible for you? There can be a world of difference between the two.

Is there any area of your life in which you are settling for second (or third) best because you figure that's the best you can pull off?

I hear the limiting phrases all the time, and years ago I used them, too:

◈ Good men are hard to find. At my age it's nearly impossible. All the good ones are taken.

◈ With my skills the best I can hope to earn is x. I don't have a degree and I've been out of the market for years taking care of the kids. There aren't many options for me.

◈ I can't seem to hold on to money. As soon as I make it, it seems to rush out of my account. I can't make it stick.

◈ My parents don't have any money and neither do I. I guess we're not the lucky ones.

What I have learned through the process of digging myself out of a large hole is that my reality is in large part influenced by my expectations. The more I raise my expectations, the more positive outcomes I seem to attract into my life.

I have come to believe that our expectations are central to our accomplishments. What we get in life is in part determined by our expectations and, by extension, our beliefs. I have experienced this over and over in my own life, and I see it play out all around me.

I HAVE COME TO BELIEVE THAT OUR EXPECTATIONS ARE CENTRAL TO OUR ACCOMPLISHMENTS.

In the opening chapter about red ribbons, I shared my story of learning to win through track-and-field. I ran as much as I could to prepare for the races. During my runs, I would play a movie in my head that looked and sounded a lot like *Chariots of Fire*, with me winning in a moment of great glory at the end. That process drilled into my brain the thought of winning and built the expectation of it. My expectations were grounded in neither reality nor reason since I knew nothing about running and had no experience. They were the result of pure imagination and desire. It worked.

Years ago my friend Suzanne shared three sentences that I've had taped to my office wall ever since:

> We subconsciously seek out what we expect.
> We get what we think we're going to get.
> We create what we think.

Most of our expectations are buried deeply within us at the subconscious level. If you want to uncover your beliefs, just take a look around you. Your life is the incarnation of your deepest beliefs about yourself. If you are surrounded by loving, supportive people, you clearly believe you are worthy of love and support. If you attract and grow money easily, then you have an abundance mentality with respect to money and believe that you are worthy of abundance.

RECALIBRATE THE INSIDE

When I started to rebuild my life, one of the first things I was told by a very successful person is that I needed to work harder on myself than on my business. Recalibrate the inside, and the outside will follow.

At first it made me mad. It sounded like a big pile of touchy-feely rubbish, so I fought it. I worked like crazy on my business—longer hours, more chasing, more reading and learning, more, more, more. What were the results? I became physically depleted and my bottom line had only inched forward. It was a ridiculously low return on my investment of time.

When I was good and tired, I gave in and started to look inside. Maybe this person, who was very successful, living a great life, knew something after all. When I stopped running and doing, turning instead to the task of figuring out my core beliefs about myself and money, I discovered a huge pile of baggage.

As we go through life, we take on emotional baggage. It all starts with our parents' beliefs about money and carries on with all of the hurt, wounds, and betrayals accumulated over the years. All of our experiences add up over time and shape our behavior, mostly in an unconscious way.

Eventually I discovered there are two kinds of expectations: those you develop consciously (that you think are running the show), and those at a deeper, subconscious level (that actually run the show). In order to change your results, you have to look at your subconscious beliefs, which frame your expectations.

UNCOVERING UNCONSCIOUS BELIEFS

So how do you discover those unconscious beliefs, you might ask? How do you know what they are? The answer I received years ago may not please you. It certainly didn't please me at the time. If you want to know what your beliefs are, just take a look at the results in your life.

> The outer conditions of a person's life will always
> be found to reflect their inner beliefs.
>
> — James Allen

Pick any area of your life—relationships, money, or health—and note what is not working for you. Since I talk about money so much, let's start with that. Let's say your financial situation is not where you'd like it to be. Here are some questions that you might ask yourself:

◈ What was I told as a child?

◈ What did I see?

⬥ What did I experience?

⬥ What are my beliefs about money and about wealthy people?

⬥ What did my parents say about money?

⬥ Was it a source of stress?

⬥ Am I comfortable talking about it, managing it, growing it? If not, which parts specifically are causing me problems?

⬥ When did my money challenges first begin? What was going on in my life at that time? With whom was I spending time, and what was their experience with money?

⬥ Do I feel hopeful and excited about where I'm headed?

⬥ If my beliefs about money were represented by a thermometer, where would my thermometer be set? Chilly or hot?

Your answers to these questions will illuminate the problem spots. There are other clues in your life, too. If you have a money-related item on your to-do list that has been there forever, that's a clue that you've got a block.

CHANGE YOUR BELIEFS AND DO THE WORK

For years after Malcolm died, I knew I should look into our stock portfolio, but I kept putting it off. For the first two years, I told myself I was grieving and had to focus on getting back on my feet. Investing was for later. Then I told myself I was too busy rebuilding to make investing a priority. I got creative about coming up with excuses about why it was never the right time to look at investments.

The ignored task weighed on me the whole time. I knew perfectly well it needed doing and was important to my future. One day I finally got mad at myself. "What is the matter with you? Why are you avoiding this? Just get on with it!" When I took a moment to think about what I was doing and why I was procrastinating about my future, I realized fear was at the bottom of it. I was afraid to consider the future because of what I had just been through. What if I created a plan and it was wiped out once again? So many bad things had happened in my personal life, and our investments seemed to mirror those results.

I was also embarrassed by what I didn't know. Surely I should know more about investing at my age? If I'm so smart, why did I not understand anything beyond superficial basics when it came to the stock market?

Then it dawned on me that I had forgotten the lessons learned so long ago on my quest for red ribbons. Back then, I worked to train myself and expected to win. Without training and belief, I would not have succeeded.

I also recalled exchanges with one of my classmates, whom I'll call Darlene, before most cross-country or track-and-field races. She would walk up to me just before the start of a race and say, "Today I'm going to beat you, Belland!" My reply was always the same: "Okay." She never did, not because she didn't have what it took to win. She was several inches taller than me and had legs that went on forever. She should have had a built-in advantage. The difference though, was that I practiced every single day when weather permitted, and I built a rock-solid belief in my ability to win. I didn't say I was going to win; I believed I would. Darlene said it but didn't believe it. Her declarations sounded like an attempt to convince herself. This is why positive affirmations alone don't work: if you don't really believe, deep down, that something is possible or probable, then it doesn't matter how often you repeat a phrase—it won't have any impact.

Once I remembered the lessons those red ribbons taught me, I made some changes. I began to read biographies of people who have had significant financial success. I wanted to know what they were doing.

It quickly became clear that real estate figures prominently in the lives of many wealthy people. Why should I reinvent the wheel? I looked around for local groups and courses, traveled to Toronto to attend a real estate investing boot camp, and read every book I could find on the subject. After several months of studying and interviewing successful investors, I began to build my portfolio.

There have been successes and failures in my real estate portfolio, but every step of the way I remind myself of my goals and reinforce my expectation of success.

Once I had developed a strong grasp of real estate investing both through my own portfolio and through the rent-to-own company I created, I finally went back to my original fear: the stock market. It was time to demystify and master this tool as well. By breaking down the barriers to real estate, I developed the confidence to study the stock market in a bid to understand its workings.

What would happen if you cranked up your expectations, even if only for your financial life? What would change if you fully expected to be wealthy, or at least wealthier than you are now? For some, it may mean never having to worry about mortgage payments or bills ever again. For others it may mean being able to be philanthropic or having the freedom to travel at will. The goal is to figure out what the stumbling blocks might be and to raise your potentially not-so-great expectations to a level that allows you to live more fully.

Oprah Winfrey gave us great advice when she said, *"Create the highest, grandest vision possible for your life, because you become what you believe."* In other words, raise your expectations and reap the benefits.

20

ILLNESS

JUDY

What would you do if you suddenly found yourself widowed with four children, the oldest of whom is seven?

Imagine yourself in the 1950s in the following situation: You're a bright, young woman working at your first job in a bank. Your father is a banker, so it seems the most natural place to be. You meet a handsome man, fall in love, and by the age of 21 you're married. A few years later you have your first child and, like most women of that generation, you walk away from your job to become a stay-at-home mom.

There is one small challenge: You don't have a driver's license. It's not that you didn't want one, you just never quite got around to it. You've practiced driving, know how it all works, but you just haven't sealed the deal officially. It's not really a problem, though, since you live in an area with good bus service. When you move to the outskirts of a larger city, your husband runs the errands and happily takes you wherever you need to go. It works fine.

Before you know it, you've got four kids and your husband has a respectable job as a school principal. No one in your community seems to have much money, yet somehow you all get by. People are resourceful and supportive.

Then comes the bombshell: you learn your husband has colon cancer and it has spread to his liver; there's nothing to be done. The next year your husband is gone and you're left alone to pick up the pieces as a solo parent of four children ranging in ages from two to seven.

Can you imagine that?

This is Judy's story. Her husband, Liam, was in great health. He played many sports, never smoked, and was by all outward appearances a healthy man. She doesn't remember him ever talking about any symptoms, but then again, you just didn't talk about things like that back then. Silence was the societal norm and your health was your own business. It was therefore not unusual for husbands and wives not to discuss their health issues.

Liam went to see his doctor when he began to experience a few unusual symptoms. To this day Judy has no idea what those symptoms were; she only knows his doctor told him he had hemorrhoids and if he lost ten pounds he would be fine. Interestingly, the diagnosis happened without an examination. In those days there were no rectal exams for such complaints.

The symptoms persisted, necessitating another trip to the doctor. This time Liam was told surgery would be required to investigate the matter further. Judy was dismayed when the surgeon told her to stay home because apparently he didn't like having to go searching for family after surgeries. She complied. During that period she relied on her parents, who had come to stay with her since she couldn't drive and had four children at home.

After the surgery Judy received a call from the doctor. In a matter-of-fact voice, he informed her of a tumor found in Liam's colon. It was clearly colon cancer. The bad news didn't end there. Three spots also presented on the liver—nothing could be done. That was it. She had just been informed over the telephone in a business-as-usual way that her husband was dying.

Liam came home in terrible shape. Since Judy couldn't drive him to the hospital, he had home care to help him deal with his colostomy bag. This proved to be difficult for him. He was a proud, private person who now found himself in a position of vulnerability that had a lot of stigma associated with it. Not only did he have to deal with devastating news, there was also the indignity of a colostomy bag. He retreated inward, never ever discussing the results or his feelings.

Judy couldn't handle the information, nor could she talk about it with Liam. It was simply too terrifying to consider. Instead, she focused on the children and on survival: diapers, meals, school, activities, and all the other facets of daily life, one day at a time.

Several months later the surgeon cut him open once again to see if the cancer had spread. Sadly, there were far fewer diagnostic tools forty years ago. It had. Once Liam heard this, he was never the same again. He went back to work as often as he could. People noticed his perseverance and his commitment, but they also noticed his deterioration. Again, Judy and Liam simply could not think about the consequences. It was all too overwhelming and frightening.

Thankfully, Judy remembered Liam did not have a will, nor did he have much life insurance. Their mortgage was in his name, and while he did have mortgage insurance, there wasn't a great deal more. They clearly couldn't alter the situation regarding life insurance, but they did need to do something about the will. They drove in silence to the lawyer's office. Every time they looked at each other, they cried, so they remained stoic and silent, each in their own separate space. It was the hardest thing they had ever done.

At the end of the school year, Liam gave the address at the graduation ceremony and died a few days later.

Judy remembers little of the days following Liam's death. She was in a state of total shock. Looking back, she has no idea how she got through that period, but she does know that family and friends stepped in to help in countless ways. Both sets of parents helped with the children and with finances. Mortgage insurance took care of her mortgage, and her father, a banker, invested the small amount of life insurance to give her a monthly income. She didn't need much to survive. Both grandfathers stepped in to act as father figures for the children for special events at school and on Father's Day. There was a tremendous amount of support.

Liam's death had left a huge hole in Judy's life. The process of grieving was a difficult one, particularly since she still had to care for four children. She worked her way through the days, and when the kids were in bed, she dissolved into tears at night. Every little thing about her life was exhausting and overwhelming, but she did it, and every time she overcame a challenge, she gained personal power and self-confidence.

There was, however, one big remaining issue no one else could solve: Judy still didn't drive. She'd had to depend on the kindness of family and friends to help her with groceries and errands since Liam's death. That clearly couldn't go on forever. Liam died at the end of June, and by July 16th Judy got her driver's license at the age of thirty-two. She could now go out on her own to buy milk.

The driver's license and the first year without Liam were a tremendous eye-opener. For years Judy had depended on Liam for so much of her life. Now, suddenly, she was in control. It was frightening, difficult—and liberating! Who knew the world was such a big place! For years Judy had been restricted to her community, to places she could easily get to on foot. When she got her driver's license, she left home and, as she puts it, she hasn't been home since! The whole year represented one liberation after another as Judy learned to take control of her life. Once you prove to yourself that you can do one minor thing, it empowers and propels you to more growth.

After such a remarkable and difficult set of experiences, it should come as no surprise that Judy has several recommendations for all women:

⬦ Don't give up your day job when you have children, even if it means working only two days per week. Having your own employment gives you confidence and contacts. It also helps to keep you up to date with any changes going on in your industry.

⬦ Change your will *every time* something significant changes in your life (e.g., medical problems, the birth of a child, a separation, and so on).

⬦ Ensure you have enough insurance to help you live beyond paying off your house.

⬦ Dig into your parents' medical history. Liam's grandfather had died of colon cancer, and yet nobody said anything until after Liam's death. If we had known, we could have insisted Liam's doctor take action at the first sign of symptoms. Knowledge is the key to prevention.

⬦ Ensure you have something to fall back on in case of a tragedy: a job, an education, and most importantly, self-confidence.

⬦ If you're going through the grieving process, be patient with yourself. It took me one year just to believe that Liam wouldn't come back and two years before I could look ahead with optimism. Grieving takes time.

HELENA

When Helena heard I was interviewing widows and divorcees for my book, she reached out to me after spending a couple of days on Parliament Hill advocating for care providers. As part of that process, she gave a speech that is so deeply touching and well written I have decided to share a portion of it with you, with her permission.

"My experience as a caregiver began innocuously: In the spring of 2006, my husband Chris complained that his hand hurt when trying to grip a golf club or throw a Frisbee. Chris was a healthy, active, forty-year-old man who had never been sick before. Chris saw our family doctor, who immediately ordered an MRI and an appointment with a neurologist.

Soon after, in July of 2006, he was officially diagnosed with ALS and told he'd likely had it for some time. He was given two years to live. At the time, our twin daughters were about to start grade three. Thus my experience as a caregiver began with no training.

In 2007, he had many falls, became significantly weaker, and began to use a motorized scooter. The following year, he required a wheelchair. The year after that, he received a ventilator and nighttime breathing equipment, and he passed away in July of 2010, approximately four years after diagnosis, the summer before the twins started grade seven.

One of Chris's wishes was to not be hospitalized. I agreed to this request and in the ensuing four years, Chris did not spend one day in the hospital. Not a single day. Instead, our home became a hospital where he could be cared for with dignity and respect for his wishes.

During this four-year period, I worked full time for about two and a half years and then took leave for one and a half years. Interestingly, I worked in the health care field, yet nothing prepared me for this experience. The people who made the biggest difference to me as a caregiver were our fabulous team of personal support workers and attendants, many of whom worked with us for two to three years and some of whom are here tonight. The consistency of this care was crucial. They are the unsung heroes of our current health care system and also deserve better treatment and more recognition.

There were many professionals involved in our home care experience. However the majority of the coordination of services and the burden of care rested squarely with me as his primary caregiver. It has been said that caregivers are the backbone of the health care system. Likewise, as a spine, I was the recipient of all the incoming messages from specialists and was the backbone of the operation, disseminating medical information and translating it into care and treatment. It required a lot of focus and energy.

Being a caregiver was by far the most difficult job I have ever undertaken. It is taxing physically, emotionally, economically, and spiritually. The toll it took to deliver 24/7 care in terms of my personal health and well-being were enormous. What got me through these dark times was the support, love, and care of our extended family, friends, and colleagues.

Their support enabled me to care for Chris. They brought our family meals, helped us adapt our home, held fundraisers, including a lavish casino night and several wine-tasting evenings and a garage sale. They set up a charitable account to help offset the costs of some of the equipment we had to purchase. They gave us air miles to reach the destinations on Chris's bucket list. One of the most poignant of the many gifts we received were donations from our daughters' school friends. These girls asked for donations to the ALS Society in lieu of receiving birthday gifts. It was heart-warming and humbling to see the compassion shown by all these amazing people. To this day, I remain truly grateful.

I needed these beautiful moments of compassion and giving. For during this time while I was taking care of Chris, I also lost both my parents and found myself being the lone parent all the time. This was an extremely challenging time for me and I felt pulled in many directions. I have always considered myself a strong and resilient person, but to tell you the truth, this nearly proved too much. Watching the man I loved struggle with the simplest things: moving his fingers, taking a breath, speaking to me, and ultimately losing even these simple abilities was both terrifying and humbling. ALS is truly a cruel disease."

In 2005, if you had asked Helena and Chris to predict what their lives would be like in the following year, their answer would certainly not have included dealing with a degenerative disease that would tear the family apart. Yet that's exactly what happened.

They had plans to travel the world together and had even lined up a year off from work to do so. Then their world turned upside down. It's unbelievable what Helena and her girls have been through in the last six years. Despite the trauma, they are doing remarkably well.

Financially, Helena is in good shape today thanks in part to the help she received from her incredible support system, but also due to her insurance coverage and her own resourcefulness. She nonetheless has several recommendations for women:

> ⬥ It is important for you to understand where your investments are, what bills you pay each month, and roughly how much you should expect to pay for utilities. I know that may sound trite, but I quite honestly had no idea and was intimidated about managing our money after so many years of leaving that to my husband.

> ⬥ Know your husband's passwords for your accounts. I had no knowledge of any of them.

> ⬥ Have a conversation with your husband about your finances and get involved right away. Luckily in my situation, my husband declined over many years and I was able to assume the role of financial manager gradually. He helped coach me on how to manage our income taxes and investments as well as how to pay the day-to-day bills and access our accounts. I do know other women who lost their husbands suddenly and found them-selves without access to money for quite some time or feeling

overwhelmed and under-prepared to face their financial future without their partner.

◈ Don't let yourself be left in the dark. Know your financial commitments each month and discuss them with your loved ones.

◈ If you have children or property, you need to ensure that you have a will so that people know what your wishes are and how you would like your assets to be distributed.

COVER YOUR ASSETS, PART II

If a child, a spouse, a life partner,
or a parent depends on you and your income,
you need life insurance.

— SUZE ORMAN

Insurance

When I began interviewing other widows about their experiences, one fact jumped out above all others: not one of the women had anticipated her husband's death. If I hadn't gone through the experience of being married to someone with a serious illness, I would probably read the stories of these women and think, "That's awful. Those poor women. Thank heavens it's not likely to happen to me." But it does happen more often than we think.

While we know women are more likely to experience divorce than the death of a spouse, the statistics are nonetheless sobering. According to the U.S. Census Bureau (1999), nearly 700,000 women lose their husbands each year and will be widows for an average of 14 years. Since women outlive men, married women will in all likelihood find themselves widowed at some point.

A third of women who become widows are younger than 60, and half of all women who will become widowed will become so by age 65 according to the Women's Institute for a Secure Retirement.

If you're one of the lucky ones who does not experience loss, then that's great. But what if it does happen to you? Would you be protected? Would you have sufficient insurance to help you get past the difficulties of dealing with loss, rebuilding your life, and thriving financially?

This issue affects women and men differently. The statistics demonstrate the skew: in 2001, the American Association of Retired Persons stated that there were 13.6 million widowed people in the United States, of whom more than 11 million were women. To put it another way, women represent the vast majority of people who are widowed.

Now let's look back at the women whose stories we've read. How did they fare with respect to life insurance?

⊗ Barbara had enough life insurance to pay off the mortgage and debts, but there was no money set aside for the twins. She says she would have been in a much better situation if they had planned their finances better and increased the amount of his life insurance policy. The amount she received helped but was inadequate. She alone carries all of the stress of raising two kids and earning money to survive.

⊗ Ann is one of the few who was in great shape. Her parents had always included her in financial discussions around budgeting. At an early age she was taught to look ahead, plan, and protect herself. Her husband had ample life insurance to leave her in a strong position and she had the skills to know what to do with the money to set herself up to thrive when she found herself alone.

⬦ Helena's husband did have life insurance, which left her in a pretty good financial situation. She also benefitted from tremendous support from her community and her own resourcefulness.

⬦ Deb's husband had a will and life insurance, so she was in reasonable financial shape after he died. She could focus on getting herself and her children through a difficult period of mourning and rebuilding.

⬦ Teresa had a mess to clean up when her husband died. First of all, there was no will, so she needed a lawyer to deal with his estate. Secondly, his estate was declared insolvent. She ended up paying thousands of dollars in legal fees. Without his income, she was maxed out with respect to cash flow and had to move out of their beloved neighborhood into a more affordable home. There was no life insurance to help deal with the situation. This was devastating for her and her children.

⬦ Cathy's husband had canceled his life insurance policy a number of years before his death without discussing it with her. They had a small child and a mortgage at the time. After he died, she inherited more than $150,000 of debts with nothing more than a bit of money from his pension to help out. She had to go back to work, in her fifties, to keep up with the bills. She will not be able to travel and enjoy retirement as she had hoped to do.

In this small sample, 50% of the women were left in reasonably stable positions financially while the other 50% either faced significant financial hardship or ended up with no protection for the future, despite having to raise young children alone. If we enlarge the sample size to include all of the women I interviewed, the vast majority of them were left in difficult situations following the death of their spouse.

According to LIMRA's Life Insurance 2013 Barometer Study, 85% of consumers agree that most people need life insurance, and yet just 62% say they have it. Of the families who have life insurance 40% don't think they have enough. (Genworth Life Jacket Study, 2011).

Since there is so much on the line if our spouse dies, why do we procrastinate when it comes to getting ample life insurance? There are a couple of possible answers. First, no one really wants to think about death. We just covered this issue in the section on wills. It is not fun to entertain the possibility of our spouse's death, so we avoid it. It's the head-in-the-sand approach.

Second, it's easier to procrastinate than to tackle an unpleasant task. The problem with procrastination is that it's easy to do, and many of us will choose the easiest path rather than tackle a challenge head-on. I know it's unpleasant to think about issues surrounding a possible death, but I can tell you it's not that much work, nor will it crush you emotionally.

When Mark and I first sat down with our lawyer to create our wills and then to calculate how much life insurance we would need, it was easier than I thought. It took some time, and we did consider a lot of unpleasant possibilities, but when it was done we both felt a tremendous sense of relief. We now knew if one of us died, the other would be left in a solid financial position and so would our children. It is a small price to pay in terms of effort and cost, given the peace of mind it brings.

I can tell you from experience that peace of mind is worth its weight in gold.

Here's a compelling story about our friend Dave regarding the importance of getting down to the business of sorting out the necessary details sooner rather than later. The email we received from him went something like this:

"My wife and I have been reading Doris's blog, and while we thought we were both on the same page regarding our situation, it turns out we weren't. As a result, we increased our insurance coverage. Several weeks later I discovered that my "widow-maker artery" was 90% blocked and I needed a stent. I had been having symptoms, but I attributed them to stress. Antacids seemed to be working, so I kept popping them back. Only after the fact did I realize how close I came to having a heart attack. I'm feeling fine now, but it was a close call.

If my wife and I hadn't stopped to consider our insurance coverage and increase it when we did, I would no longer be eligible because I now have a heart condition."

Dave and his family are protected because they took action right away. They had no idea a heart problem was brewing. It was all the more surprising since there is no history of heart disease in the family and, while Dave isn't an athlete, he is in decent shape and takes good care of himself.

I know what it's like to survive a loss without insurance. Malcolm was not insurable because of his cancer. At one point he even tried to have his right hand insured since he was an artist, but no company would touch him, not even his hand! When he died, there was no money to help out. I lost his productive income while inheriting all of the bills and debts we had amassed together for our business. The funeral alone cost several thousand dollars even with a simple pine box and cremation.

Gail Vaz-Oxlade, a financial writer and speaker, has blunt advice for people who are "too cheap" to pay for life insurance which goes something like this: You can pay a small price now for peace of mind, or you can pay the price later after your husband has died and you're left with a ton of financial stress.

If you're unwilling to buy insurance for yourself, think of your children and of ensuring they have a solid future if the worst happens.

Credit Score

This area is often overlooked when women think about their financial health, and yet it has a significant impact when you need to borrow money.

If we boil financial success down to the first key stepping stone, it all starts with a rock-solid credit profile. Why? Because that's the way the world measures how creditworthy you are. If you live a 100% cash lifestyle and never borrow money or sign up for any services, you won't need a credit score. In all other instances, your score will come into play, affecting the number of options you'll have. If something should happen to your spouse and suddenly you're on your own, it will be essential to have a good score.

So just who uses your score to evaluate you? Here is a partial list:

⬦ Lenders and banks, when you want to buy a house or get a loan of any kind, and they keep checking for the term of the loan. If your score dips too low, they can call in the loan or refuse to renew, or increase the interest rate on your line of credit.

⬦ Car companies, when you want to obtain financing. Unless you have a pocket full of cash to pay for that new or new-to-you car, you're going to need a loan from someone.

⬦ Insurance companies, when you want to insure a house or a car. A cash lifestyle won't help you here. They may refuse to insure you if your score is too low, or they will charge you much higher premiums. You will pay dearly for a bad score.

⬦ Employers. Some of them check to see how creditworthy you are. It gives them an idea of your risk profile. Are you the kind of person who doesn't pay your bills on time? Some employers want to know.

❖ Credit card companies check every time you apply for a card, and they keep checking the entire time you have the card.

❖ Landlords. If you want to rent an apartment, you often have to give consent for the landlord to check your credit. They want to know that you pay your bills on time. No consent, no rental.

❖ Cell phone companies. We all love to hate them, but the fact remains that the vast majority of adults have a cell phone. Cell phone providers pull your credit before agreeing to sign you up for a plan, and they will be merciless if you don't pay your bills on time.

Do you need a good credit score to invest in stocks, bonds, and Guaranteed Investment Certificates? No. How about investing in real estate? Your score will matter a great deal if you want to be on Title, but it is not necessary if you simply want to lend money as a money partner on a deal or as a second mortgage holder.

Do you need a good score to set up a savings account? No, you don't. So you can clearly save and invest in some assets without a good score, but heaven help you if you ever want or need to borrow money. And you *will* need to borrow money at some point.

Think of your credit score as the foundation of your financial house. With a strong score, you can build a large financial structure and have options when trouble hits.

I have co-written an eBook with my friend and business colleague Sandra Tisiot entitled *Improve Your Credit Score, Fix Issues, and Avoid Bad Habits*. You can obtain a free copy on my website at www.doris belland.com/creditscore.

Here is a brief summary of what a good score looks like and the factors that influence it:

⬧ Target a Beacon score of 680 or greater. (This applies to Canada. If you're from another country, I suggest you look into the details for your credit-reporting agencies.)

⬧ Have at least two trade lines (e.g., credit cards or loans) with a $2,000 credit limit each. You can have a higher limit if you like, but it's not necessary. With a higher limit, I ask only one question: How are you using that credit? If the answer is "wisely," then terrific. If not, you may want to rethink the credit limit and ask for a decrease.

⬧ Do not carry any credit card debt, as it will erode your wealth with those crazy interest rates. If you absolutely must carry credit card debt for a short while, then keep your balances below 35% of your credit limit. I know that some clever people will say, "Hey, no problem. To maintain my ratios, I'll just crank up my limit!" Sure, you can do that, if you'd like to go broke faster. If you're looking for ways to carry more debt, think again. Rule #1: no credit card debt.

⬧ Pay all bills on time, every time. This is a really big deal, particularly if you've had serious credit issues in the past. Lenders are not forgiving when it comes to late payments after you've been through a bankruptcy or a consumer proposal. Every late payment will show up on your record and will stay there for several years. (The precise length of time varies by credit-reporting agency.)

So what sorts of things hurt your credit score? Here's a quick list:

⬧ Spending more than your credit limit and carrying high balances.

⬧ Paying late. Automate all payments to ensure that you never miss a bill.

❖ Too many inquiries on your file.

❖ Collections. You can argue about a bill all you like, but if you don't pay it, the company will likely send it to collections or report it directly to the credit reporting agencies, all of which will show up on your bureau. Then the collection stays on your bureau for years. Cell phone companies are notorious for this. Pay the bill, and then fight it out with them. It's frustrating, I know, but that's how it works.

It's a good idea to check your credit report once a year to ensure there are no errors. If you've been through some rough times and your report looks like a dog's breakfast, don't give up. Every single credit issue can be fixed with time and determination. It's worth the effort.

If you don't know how to interpret your credit report, reach out to an experienced mortgage broker for help. They should be able to explain what everything means and how it works.

Credit Cards and Co-signing for Loans

If I had a dollar for every credit file I've seen in which one partner gets stuck with the ex-partner's spending spree, I'd have an even healthier investment fund by now. It happens all the time.

Most of the damaged credit files that come across my desk are the result of divorce, with an honorable mention going to poor spending choices. Here's a common scenario: both partners have joint credit cards. One person racks up the bills and takes off, leaving the other to pick up the financial pieces. Unfortunately, the lenders will go after both parties on the contract regardless of who created the debt in the first place.

In other situations, one person in a couple has great income but terrible credit whereas the other, often the woman, has a much lower income but good credit. She co-signs on a loan because she can use her credit to obtain the loan; then she's left responsible for the debt when things go south and her partner stops paying. It can be devastating financially to get stuck with the debt on a fraction of your ex's income.

The way to protect yourself is to be discriminating about co-signing for loans. This is the time to set aside emotions and ask yourself whether the loan is wise and the risk is reasonable. Ask what's in it for you and what would happen if the relationship went south. If your boyfriend can't get a loan for a new car without your help, that's his issue, not yours. Don't make yourself vulnerable by taking on other people's financial issues.

Where possible, keep debts separate. As much as you may love your partner, joint credit cards and loans are a liability. If you're buying a house or investment properties together, that's one thing, but in every case evaluate the risk carefully. Joint debt can really hurt you, both in the event of a breakdown in the relationship or the death of your partner.

Also, ensure your name shows up on as many assets as possible. In this case, my definition of an asset is the one presented by Robert Kiyosaki in his book *Rich Dad, Poor Dad,* if only to get you thinking about assets, liabilities, and cash flow. An asset is something that puts money in your pocket. By this definition, a car is not an asset.

If you get your name on the assets and off the liabilities, you're off to a good start. You may nonetheless choose to share various liabilities with your spouse, but the key is to make conscious choices with an awareness of the benefits and the potential risks involved. Eyes wide open on this one.

Passwords

A couple of my friends wanted to pick my brain about how protected I thought they were. There were somber looks when I asked a few uncomfortable questions, including, "Do you know your husband's passwords?" The short answer was no. If something were to happen to their spouses, they wouldn't have the faintest idea how to get into his files or even know what to look for. Nor did they have a good grasp of the family's investments.

From what I'm hearing as I speak with women, my friends are not alone. Take a moment to think about your situation. How would you fare if your spouse disappeared tomorrow? Would you be able to easily access all of your accounts, including his? Do you know all of the passwords? Are you aware of all of your banking and investment details?

The answer for most of us is no. Sure, we know there are files for everything (maybe) and that passwords are kept on various post-it notes/ memo pads/printed lists hidden somewhere clever (if only you knew where that was). But for many of us, if we had to retrieve all of the information tomorrow, we would be in a bind. Now add the stress of an emotional situation, and you've got a recipe for a whole lot of pain.

The first issue we face is the sheer number of passwords most of us have. Trying to remember them all is like trying to memorize *Ulysses*— cool if you can pull it off but not likely to happen.

My husband, Mark, is gravely concerned about online security. It made him crazy that I was not exactly diligent about ensuring all accounts have strong, unique passwords. He repeatedly told me about a clever tool, LastPass, that takes on the issue of multiple, insecure passwords. LastPass is one example of several such tools that exist to generate strong, random passwords for all of your accounts, and then keep track of them all. You just need to remember one master password to get into LastPass (or another similar tool) in the first place. This also means that if your husband uses the same system, you need to know only a single password to access his information.

I wish I could say the minute Mark told me about LastPass, I immediately recognized the brilliance of the system and hopped on board. Not quite. Mark repeatedly told me about it, and every time I'd reply, "Yes, very clever—I'll get right on it." He eventually installed it on my computer, spent ten minutes showing me how to use it, and then waited patiently for my sheepish admission that I should have done this ages ago.

It works. And now that I know Mark's LastPass password, I can access all of his accounts if something happens to him. There is one password to memorize. No more excuses.

Now, just because you know the password(s) to get into your spouse's accounts doesn't mean you know what's actually in there. It's a good idea to sit down on a regular basis to go over all of your financial information and review the accounts: what investments and debts do you have?

My business colleague Sandra developed a clever organizational tool called *My Life Locker*. She had become sick and tired of having to ferret around in multiple places to find documents and personal information. She looked everywhere for a product to help her keep important information in one location, but nothing existed. So she created one. Sandra recently sold the electronic rights to *My Life Locker*. It is now available online through www.LegalWills.ca for $29.95 (at time of publication). You can use my discount code—THRIVE20—for a 20% discount. All profits from my affiliate link to *My Life Locker* will be invested in courses to grow women's financial literacy.

Something Sandra said to me a long time ago has stayed with me: "We are moved by inspiration or desperation." One is a lot easier to deal with than the other.

22

ABUSE

SARAH

Sarah and John were an impressive couple living what appeared to be a great life: she had a management-track job with a large IT company, and he was a successful academic researcher. They both had strong salaries and promising prospects. The path ahead, personally and professionally, appeared to be golden.

For the first six years they lived together as a common-law couple but, despite outward appearances, all was not well. Sarah soon discovered John had multiple lovers. She comes from a deeply religious background in which commitment and forgiveness are central tenets, so she stayed with John. However, her willingness to turn the other cheek ended the day she discovered he had proposed to one of his lovers. She asked him to leave.

The year they were apart, she made what she calls her first critical mistake. John had called and asked to see her again. His appeals sounded genuine and heartfelt, so she agreed to meet him. One thing led to another and they became intimate that evening. The next day she realized this was not the path she wanted, and she chose to carry on alone.

It had been a promising year for Sarah. She had bought a house, pursued her own interests, and continued to thrive at work. Financial security had been a big issue for her, so it was all the more satisfying when she was finally on her way to establishing a life of comfort and security.

All that changed the day that she discovered she was pregnant.

Scores of women around the world choose to raise a child alone; that's not unusual, however, Sarah faced significant road blocks in trying to choose that path for herself. First, her deeply religious family pressured her to marry John "for the sake of the child" and, really, for the preservation of appearances. John's family, who were also religious, did the same. To make matters worse, Sarah's employer made it clear that unwed mothers were frowned upon in the company and if she persisted as a solo parent her management-track position would be at risk. One manager effectively told her if she refused to marry the father of the child, she would be relegated to menial work with no hope of promotion. Consequently her income would plummet.

In case you're wondering if this happened in a third-world country, the answer is no. It happened in Canada in a large, well-known company in the 2000s. Today, Sarah knows she should have held her ground and followed her own heart, but back then, she was afraid of losing her job and financial security. She caved to the pressure and married John. Days before the wedding, she miscarried the child. By then she felt stuck; she felt obliged to go through with the wedding.

Over the following several years, Sarah was pregnant eleven times; nine pregnancies ended in miscarriage, one child was stillborn, and another survived for only one month after being born premature. The toll on Sarah's physical and emotional health was enormous. After the heartbreak of repeated failure, they adopted a child from another country.

All this time, John's behavior worsened, ranging from emotionally abusive to physically intimidating. Financially, there was a lot of stress for Sarah as well because, despite John's excellent salary, he was not contributing at all to the household costs, including the mortgage. His attitude appeared to be that Sarah's money was theirs, but his money was exclusively his. At one point, he was involved in a lawsuit and expected Sarah to resolve it by paying $30,000 from her savings. She refused.

As Sarah describes it, she spent her thirties paying off their home with the expectation it would bring her some financial slack, which would in turn allow her to focus on raising their daughter. That proved to be an exercise in futility.

The breaking point came when Sarah suffered a health crisis. In a fit of rage, John beat the family dog in front of their daughter as Sarah lay helpless in bed, recovering from surgery. That was a defining moment for her. She was now afraid for their daughter, and she realized she had no future with this man.

Sadly the worst of John's behavior was yet to come, as Sarah discovered after she asked him to leave. Now he was furious.

It's often said that money doesn't make you a good or bad person, it just enhances the kind of person you already are. In the right hands, money can be transformative. The same holds true of money in the wrong hands.

In the last few months of the marriage, John came into an inheritance. This was before Sarah asked him for a divorce. When it became clear their marriage was over, John transferred the funds to a family member so that Sarah could not go after it as part of the divorce. As Sarah points out, she had no designs on his inheritance. During their seventeen years together, she had never once asked him for money.

The inheritance, coupled with John's strong income and the fact that he had not paid any household costs for years, provided him with a large pool of money with which to go after Sarah. And he did. He engaged lawyers to fight every conceivable battle, forcing Sarah to chew through her savings. Every conversation involved a lawyer at $350 per hour. To date, Sarah has spent more than $100,000 on legal bills, and sadly, the fight isn't over. John keeps finding more issues to raise in order to drag her into yet another battle. Sarah knows these battles won't end for many years until their daughter is an adult and can no longer be used as a pawn to get to her. He appears to be intentionally setting out to destroy her as punishment for walking away from him.

The price Sarah has paid goes well beyond the fees paid to lawyers. First, the constant court dates have cost Sarah her job. She has become a consultant in order to have the flexibility to address all of the ongoing issues and, not surprisingly, her income has suffered. So has her quality of life. She can no longer afford many of the basics she used to take for granted. When I asked Sarah what she is doing differently as a result of her lifestyle changes, the list went from cutting her own hair and making her own bread to cycling everywhere to cut down on costs.

Sarah has some challenging years ahead and yet, despite the heaviness of her situation, she is remarkably positive. The health crisis she experienced as a result of overwhelming stress was a wake-up call for her to celebrate life, and she has gone on to pursue athletics she otherwise would never have entertained. To hear her speak is an inspiration, particularly in light of her living conditions. One can't help but be impressed by the depth of her strength.

It's that very strength that prompted me to ask a difficult question: how was it possible for John to dominate her in the way that he did? By any measure, Sarah is a highly intelligent, strong, capable woman. How did this happen?

There is no easy answer. If anything, the answer is possibly "one small action at a time." You allow one problem to go unchecked, and then another develops, and before you know it, your world is a complicated mess. It happens all the time.

Sarah's first piece of advice to all women is: "Your truth is your truth. Follow your heart and don't let anyone pressure you into a decision that doesn't feel right for you. I should never have married John, regardless of the societal consequences. It was a terrible decision for me. Make your own decisions."

Here is a list of recommendations she wishes she had followed herself:

⬧ Understand that marriage is a financial partnership. Don't marry someone you could never do business with.

⬧ If you are bringing different assets into the marriage (e.g., a house), sign a prenuptial agreement.

⬧ You can survive as a self-employed, single parent. Don't let fear drive your decision-making.

⬧ Ask for financial statements or discovery at the beginning of a relationship, and understand what assets and liabilities your partner is bringing into the union.

⬧ Keep in mind that many promises never materialize. "Later" never comes; there is only today's actions and deeds.

⬧ Ask yourself, "Am I modeling behavior I want to see in my children?" If not, make changes to your situation.

RITA

Interviewing Rita was like getting a lesson in the history of Eastern Europe from the time of some of the original James Bond stories. She grew up behind the Iron Curtain, where information about the world was controlled, poverty was widespread, and opportunities for a good life were few and far between. As she explains it, the rules were different in her old world. When she eventually made it to Canada, she thought she had arrived to the land of joy and opportunity. She had, but as with many such stories, there is a sad, unexpected twist.

From a young age, Rita showed signs of strength and self-determination. She decided to go to college to study computing science, something uncommon for women even today in North America, let alone in an Eastern European country a few decades ago.

While in college, she became pregnant and, unfortunately for her, the father of the child had no desire to get married, nor did he contribute any money for the child's care. Her family, instead of being a source of great support, shunned her because she was now an unwed mother, a shameful state in that country at the time. Rita was left alone with her child to complete her university degree and to earn money as best she could. It was such a stressful time that, to this day, Rita cannot recall when she graduated. It's all a blur.

After a couple of years of working and living on her own, Rita was desperate to get married. Life as an unwed mother was indeed difficult in her society and it became clear that to have any hope of getting ahead, she needed a husband.

She met her husband-to-be, Michael, on an out-of-town business trip. For him it was love at first sight and he proposed three days later. For her, however, he was the antithesis of the man she thought she'd marry: he had dropped out of high school, was uneducated, he was bald, and he didn't have a great job. At first, she took no notice of him, but eventually she realized he was a genuine soul with a good heart, so she agreed to marry him.

Rita was now in a decent position personally. Michael was so kind and warm, she eventually grew to love him. Given her new respectability, her family once again acknowledged her existence. She and Michael had a child together, a second daughter for Rita, and settled into a reasonably contented home life.

Professionally, however, Rita was stuck. In order to marry Michael, she had to move to his village in Ukraine, a place with a population of roughly two thousand people. It was a stark contrast to her previous urban existence and provided a real challenge for her: what on earth would she do for a job? She was a computer programmer who now found herself in a small, rural village.

She did the only thing she knew how to do: she computerized the village. In the process she developed a successful business that was highly regarded by the locals. That was fine for a few years, but eventually she yearned for more. In the village everyone was poor and the shops were empty. Everywhere she looked, she saw nothing but a bleak future for herself and her daughters. Two generations of women in her family had waited for a better life that never came, and now Rita saw herself following the same path.

Her boredom and dissatisfaction eventually led her to consider emigrating, but where could she go? Behind the Iron Curtain, there was little information available on other countries. At the time, only three countries to her knowledge were accepting immigrants: Australia, New Zealand, and Canada. The first two were too far away and contained far too many bugs, something she dreaded. She chose Canada for its twin virtues of being closer and having fewer bugs. Rita clearly hadn't yet experienced the woods in Canada in June.

Without telling anyone, she applied and was accepted for a visa to Canada. For the next two years, Rita worked diligently and managed to raise the money she needed to emigrate. During that time her husband did not believe she would go through with it. When she eventually raised the needed capital, they had a frank conversation that resulted in an ultimatum: he could stay if he chose to, but she was taking the girls to Canada. It was only then that he fully understood the extent of her resolve. The only thing they needed now was to purchase the plane tickets.

Unfortunately, Michael had not heeded Rita's advice to be discreet about their plans, and the local KGB found out they were planning to leave. They started following Michael and Rita. It became obvious that trouble was brewing when one of the officials called Rita in for questioning.

The official made it clear that if they attempted to leave, a confession containing Rita's forged signature would be used to have Michael jailed.

Rita rushed home, packed two handbags, and left with her husband and daughters, abandoning their house. They stayed with relatives in another town until the police showed up at their door. The relatives lied to the police while the family hid under a bed upstairs.

As soon as the police left, they fled to a hotel near the airport in Kiev, where they hid while waiting for plane tickets to arrive. They did not leave the room except to get food once a day. The wait was agonizing. Would the police find them? Would the police think to notify the airport? Would they be stopped before boarding the plane? They waited and worried. Eventually the tickets arrived, and they got on the plane without difficulty, but the stress of being chased like criminals haunted Rita for years. To this day Rita still has no idea why they were upset that two of their residents were emigrating to Canada.

At long last, Rita was back in a large city in a country that offered countless opportunities. It was a dream come true and she worked hard to integrate as quickly as possible. She updated her skills, took more English classes, and soon got a job as a computer programmer.

Michael did not fare as well. Back in Ukraine they had made a good team in their business, but she had been the driving force for the enterprise. In Canada, he was rudderless. Despite daily English lessons, he still couldn't speak a word of the language eighteen months later and was therefore unemployable. His whole world revolved around waiting for Rita and his daughters to come home. He had made a few friends in the ex-pat community, but they only served to reinforce his sense of alienation. Rita was expanding her world while he regressed in his.

After a couple of years of watching Michael make no progress despite her repeated attempts to help, Rita's opinion of him lessened, and resentment grew. She eventually made the difficult decision to leave him, a choice which shocked and angered Michael. He argued with her, trying desperately to get her to change her mind. When it was clear she was determined, something snapped in him. He came into her bedroom while she was sleeping, jumped on the bed, and began to strangle her. He said she belonged to him and that if he couldn't have her, no one else would. Despite their size difference, Rita managed to get him off her long enough to cry out and talk to him. He changed his mind: instead of strangling her, he raped her.

Rita was an emotional mess with no one to turn to. After days of crying at work, she finally confided to a colleague, who urged Rita to call the police. Charges were pressed and Michael was hauled off to jail. Then guilt set in.

Rita felt so bad about Michael's being in jail that she bailed him out. He resumed his behavior, telling Rita, "You're not leaving me. I'll follow you wherever you go." At this point Rita knew she needed to escape and, thanks to her boss, she was relocated to another city. Michael discovered she was leaving only when the moving van arrived at their house. Under the watchful protection of the workers, Rita left with her girls.

For the third time in her life, Rita began rebuilding her life from scratch in a new home. Everything was going brilliantly until she began to have feelings of guilt about the girls never seeing their father. Why should they be deprived of him? After all, he was fundamentally a good man who had snapped under extreme duress. At his core, he was a good guy. She called him and offered him the opportunity to visit the girls, reiterating, however, that they would never again be together. This was being done for the sake of the girls. Michael agreed and a meeting was arranged.

Once Michael arrived at Rita's house, he refused to leave. Rita called the police and they escorted Michael out of her house. One week later, there was a knock on her door in the middle of the night. It was the police. They told her that Michael had committed suicide.

In that moment, Rita's world fell apart. She had been through so much already and now she felt partly responsible for her husband's death. More than a decade later, she is still overcome with emotion as she recounts her story. It doesn't help that all of her friends and family from back home blamed her for leaving, as did the ex-pats whom she had befriended. Only her Canadian friends were understanding of her need to leave Michael. Rita's experience has clearly left her scarred.

THIS IS A COMMON TRAIT IN THE MAJORITY OF THE WOMEN I HAVE INTERVIEWED—THE DISBELIEF THAT ANYTHING OF THE SORT COULD HAPPEN TO THEM.

When I asked her if she would have done anything differently had she known what would happen, she insists she would not have believed it. This is a common trait in the majority of the women I have interviewed—the disbelief that anything of the sort could happen to them.

Since Rita was the bread-winner for the family, she is not bereft as a result of Michael's death. That said, she does point out that she did not understand the concept of insurance. There was no such thing in her country, therefore, when it was presented as an option here, she simply filled out "$10,000" when asked how much insurance she wanted for Michael. It seemed like a large amount at the time. Had she fully understood its importance, she would have significantly increased her coverage and left herself and her daughters in much better financial shape.

Her recommendations below apply to all women, not just immigrants:

⬧ Set up a network of friends outside your cultural community. Otherwise, you may be isolated when you go against the grain of the community's norms.

⬧ Don't let pride prevent you from reaching out for help. Pride helped me become strong and independent, but it also hurt me at key moments.

⬧ Get the support you need. Ask your friends and colleagues for recommendations and reach out for support. There is no need to try to cope or adapt alone.

JEAN

When we marry, we typically promise to love our spouse in sickness and in health, but one never imagines that sickness will descend into destruction and abuse requiring legal intervention.

Jean and Henry were a normal couple for whom everything seemed to progress as you might expect. They were married in the summer of 1972 and had four children in reasonably quick succession. Jean has a master's degree in environmental science and Henry was the vice-principal at a school in a large city. He was also a well-respected and well-known member of their community. Initially, Jean worked in her field, but as her family grew, she stepped away from work to care for the children.

Life was not without its challenges in those early days. Henry's position brought with it tremendous stress, which was exacerbated by long commutes in rush-hour traffic. While he was quite active, he was also a smoker. The pressure at work, combined with his smoking habit and a type A personality, eventually took its toll.

In 1978, on his thirty-eighth birthday, Henry had a heart attack. He survived, but the two-week stay in the hospital as well as his doctor's orders to stop all activities, marked the start of a downward spiral.

For many of us, it takes a medical emergency to make us realize how unprepared we are. The same was true for Henry. However, he was in for another shock. He wanted life insurance to protect his family, but due to his heart attack, he was no longer eligible. He decided to invest in real estate to compensate for the lack of insurance. What he could not have foreseen was that interest rates would soon skyrocket into double digits. When that happened, the family had to declare bankruptcy and in the process, they lost everything. That was in 1988.

Jean tells a heartbreaking story of the day the bailiff came to repossess the van. Their oldest child was home at the time and saw it all.

Between Henry's heart attack and the real estate fiasco, there was another tragic event. Exactly one year after Henry's heart attack, things went from bad to much worse when Jean and Henry lost a baby boy in childbirth. The baby was full term, but tragically he died from a complication. Both Jean and Henry were devastated by the loss.

Jean describes the aftermath of losing the baby as brutal. Henry, who was already suffering from depression, sank further and further into a psychological black hole. As back-to-back tragedies struck, he turned to alcohol as a coping mechanism.

From 1980 to 1988, Henry drank more and more until he was considered an alcoholic and had cirrhosis of the liver. After they declared bankruptcy in 1988, Jean went back to work and Henry had a breakdown. The final blow to his ego came when he was removed from his job and placed on disability. His behavior quickly descended into verbal abuse. It was an awful time for Jean and the children, who were all, in their own way, traumatized by Henry's behavior.

The family situation spiralled further downward. As Jean worked harder and harder to keep her family together, Henry, who felt increasingly guilty and angry, drank more.

The breaking point came in 1990, when Henry threw all of Jean's possessions on the front lawn while three of the children watched from inside the house. At that moment, Jean knew she had to make a choice between Henry and the kids. After years of trying to deal with the abuse on her own, she finally succumbed and called the police. It was humiliating for everyone. First, Henry was a well-known and well-respected man who had gone downhill. Second, you can imagine the trauma of having all of your things strewn about the lawn with police cars parked in front of your house and officers dragging your husband away in front of the kids and the neighbors. Dreadful—there's just no other way to describe it.

The episode led to a restraining order, which Henry tested on a couple of occasions. After being evicted from the house, Henry slept under bridges for a time and yet continued to sing in the church choir. As Jean describes it, he was in complete denial, a textbook alcoholic.

At home meanwhile, Jean was trying to pick up the pieces for her family. She and the children had all been deeply affected by Henry's alcoholism. The kids had to develop coping mechanisms to deal with their father's illness, not to mention the societal stigma of having a father at home. Jean spent a lot of time during the 1990s trying to help her children to understand how their father was ill and that they shouldn't hate him.

It all ended for Henry in 1996, when he succumbed to his disease. For Jean, there was finally a measure of relief. Quite understandably, she had wished him dead on many occasions. On that point there was some closure, but unfortunately the effects of years of abuse and trauma persisted for the family.

Two of the children are in therapy to this day to deal with the impact of their father's alcoholism. One child also had a heart attack when she was 38. The family have all paid a heavy price for their father's illness.

Today Jean feels she enabled Henry. She used to find bottles and would make excuses to protect the kids. Since she had no experience with alcoholism, she didn't know how far it would go. When he would refrain from alcohol for a while, she believed that things would work out. When he started drinking again, she kept telling herself he would and could get better. Through it all, there was a desperate grasping for hope.

I asked Jean if she ever thought of leaving Henry. The thought of divorce had been too scary with four kids. It was such a busy time that she didn't think she could manage on her own. In addition, she wanted to try to preserve the family and his reputation, too. Divorce was unpalatable on so many levels.

Jean has learned a great deal as a result of her experiences and has the following advice for women:

◇ Don't wear rose-colored glasses. It's fine to be optimistic, but there's a point at which you have to be honest with yourself about your situation. It does you no good to lie to yourself.

◇ Your response to situations will determine your outcome. You want to be able to look back without regret. Take a good, long look at the situation you face, and have the courage to make the best choice.

◇ Whatever your situation, you have the strength to cope. Just have faith in yourself and get support in various forms.

◇ There are some things about your spouse that you can never change. Don't delude yourself, otherwise, you might enable destructive behavior.

As I ended my interview with Jean, I was struck by how determined and practical she is despite everything she's been through. She is a great example of the boundless supply of strength and resilience in all women.

THE GARBAGE MAN AND THE GUN

Risk comes from not knowing
what you're doing.

— WARREN BUFFETT

I attended a talk given by Dr. Daniel Levitin, professor of Psychology and Behavioral Neuroscience at McGill University, in which he shared a funny story. Some years ago he was at a party where a colleague of his mentioned he was looking to buy a new car. When Dr. Levitin asked him what he had in mind, the colleague went on at great length about the research he'd done and which car had the best safety, reliability, and performance statistics. After reviewing reams of research from reputable sources, he had figured out which car he was going to buy; he just hadn't gotten around to it yet.

Sometime later Dr. Levitin crossed paths with his colleague once again, and he asked him about his new car: "Are you enjoying Car X?" Came the reply, "I didn't end up buying X. I bought Z instead." Dr. Levitin was surprised. "But your research and careful analysis clearly showed that

Car X is superior. What made you change your mind?" His colleague replied, "Oh, I spoke to my uncle, who had owned Car X, and he told me he had had nothing but problems with it, so I bought Z instead."

One uncle, one data point, and there went a ton of careful research out the window! Bias and emotions can do quite a number on decision-making.

I can't criticize Dr. Levitin's colleague because I did exactly the same thing—I ignored my own research and systems—at a critical time, too—except in my case, the consequences were much more significant.

Anyone plugged in to the world of neuroscience knows that emotions play a key role in our decision-making, whether we like it or not. If you watch skillful negotiators, they don't spend their time rolling out strictly logical arguments—they tap into the other party's emotions.

I'm certainly not about to make the case that we need to keep emotions out of decision-making, because research shows it's impossible. What I will say, though, is that allowing pure emotions to take over and ignoring what you know can be a costly mistake.

The lesson I'm about to share has nothing to do with my loss of Malcolm; it came several years later. However, it is one of the bigger lessons I have learned in the process of rebuilding my professional life, so I want to share it.

In 2005 I decided to develop a real estate portfolio. I read everything I could get my hands on, interviewed successful investors with large portfolios, and developed sound business systems based on an intensive training course given by a group of experienced investors.

Later that year, after looking at dozens of potential investment properties, I bought the first one, a triplex, in an area of transition in Ottawa. On one side of the area, there is one of the most expensive, exclusive neighborhoods in this city, while on the other, you find a mix of blue-collar workers, retirees living in modest homes, drug dealers, and prostitutes. Our property was pretty much on the dividing line, so we figured that we could still attract decent tenants with attractive rents.

The property performed well for the first year, and when the tenant in the three-bedroom unit moved out, we took that opportunity to do some renovations in order to get rid of the tragic décor. A few months later, we put it out on the market for rent and. . . nothing. We had a few couples walk through the place, including some diplomats, but it wasn't a fit for them.

Then, during one of the showings, a mom came in with her two boys. She loved the place. More to the point, her two boys loved the place and made it sound like this would be the first time in their life that they could each have their own bedroom. Mom, whom I'll call Sheila, filled out the application form on the spot and started to tell me her life story.

She was a single mom to the two boys, whose father had walked out on them when they were babies. Since then she had worked hard to raise the boys and ensure they had a good future. Up until recently she had worked at a good office job, but since she had gone back to school to improve her skills, she had left that job and taken on a waitressing job for greater flexibility with hours. While she brought in enough money for the rent and other expenses, she recognized this might be a little risky for me, so her parents were willing to co-sign the lease.

When I did a credit check I found exactly what she said I'd find: a mess. She had gone through hell when the children's father left, and as a result, her credit was in terrible shape. Still, she was definitely back on track. Her previous landlord had given her a good recommendation and said she'd left only because the place was too small for her and the boys. Her boss at the restaurant confirmed she had been working there for the past year and did a good job, and she provided a letter from a local college saying she had been accepted into a business administration program.

Something didn't add up, though. The number she gave me for her landlord was a cell number, not a land line. Today that's common, but back then it wasn't. Why just a cell phone? And the credit file was dreadful. Could this woman really be trusted? Could she really afford a three-bedroom apartment or was it too much for a single mom?

I spoke to her parents and they confirmed they would certainly co-sign for their daughter. She had been through so much, and they just wanted to secure a good home for their daughter and grandkids.

As I evaluated Sheila's application, my head kept screaming to say no in a hurry. This was a big mess waiting to happen, but my heart hijacked the conversation. At the time, I had a three-year-old daughter and was five months pregnant with my second daughter. My head told me in no uncertain terms to walk away from this woman, but my mom heart-strings pulled me to override all rational concerns. Everyone deserves a break, right? Surely I could do my bit to help out a fellow mom raising her kids alone. Those poor boys had endured so much already. Could I really turn them away? After all, the parents were co-signing. Surely everything would work out well.

Despite all of my reservations, I said yes.

Sheila was effusive in her gratitude. Finally someone was giving her a chance, and thank you so much. Yes, of course she would maintain the yard to which she had exclusive access and yes, indeed she would meet all other requirements. No problem.

One month after she moved in, the problems began.

Her second rent check bounced. When I called her she was terribly embarrassed.

"So sorry, there was a problem at the bank." She was in the process of changing accounts and the money hadn't been moved over yet. She would get me the money in a couple of days.

Then the next check bounced as well. That's when I knew I was going to have a hard time with her. This time she told me her hours had been reduced temporarily at work but everything would be fine next month and could she pay me in installments?

A couple of weeks later, as I was trying to chase her for the rent money, I got a call from a police officer.

"There's been an incident with one of the tenants at your unit."

Apparently her boyfriend (what boyfriend?) had pulled a gun on the garbage collector because he was asked to move his car, which was blocking access to the driveway. The boyfriend apparently fled and was now on the police's wanted list.

A meeting with the police also revealed they had been watching my building because they suspected Sheila was selling drugs.

At this point a few months had gone by, and I had served the tenant with the proper notices stating she had to pay up or be evicted. I heard nothing. Every time I drove by, the curtains were drawn and there was no sign of life. I finally left a notice taped to the door stating I would be entering the next day to inspect the unit.

When I showed up, the note was still taped to the door. I knocked on the door and rang the doorbell. Nothing. When I unlocked the door and began to open it, her two large dogs lunged at me, growling and baring their teeth. I just managed to get the door shut in time to avoid the dogs. At this point I was eight months pregnant, so moving with speed wasn't always easy. The dogs continued to throw themselves at the door as I hurried to secure the deadbolt. I was petrified.

I called the Humane Society and waited in my car for them to arrive. I also called a large friend who graciously came out immediately to be with me as I entered the premises. The Humane Society staff managed to subdue and remove the dogs, photograph the environment, and take a statement from me. Then I was allowed into the unit. What my friend and I saw when we finally gained access was shocking.

Sheila had clearly left in a hurry with her boys, abandoning her two dogs in the apartment. She had left large bags of food on the floor of the kitchen and the basement. The toilet, with its seat raised, was their only source of water. I guessed the dogs had been alone in the apartment for roughly three weeks. They appeared to be physically fine, but they were not happy.

When the Humane Society workers removed the animals, we were left with a shattered unit: dog feces *everywhere,* chewed wood and claw marks on most of the door frames and doors, children's clothes, toys, and sports equipment scattered about, a fridge full of rotting food, and more junk than I have ever seen strewn on every surface both inside and out. I can remember needing to sit down from the shock of it all, but not daring to touch any surface. Every square inch was disgusting.

When we turned to the parents for help, we discovered they were mentally disabled—high functioning but mentally disabled nonetheless—and while their credit was good, they were essentially penniless. What little money they did have their daughter stole from them on her way out of town. It was a tragic situation in every conceivable way.

That mistake cost us more than twelve thousand dollars and a lot of heartache. This is how I spent the first few months of my youngest daughter's life, and all because I let emotions alone guide my decision-making at the outset.

Or so I thought until I came across Eric Barker's blog post entitled *This Is How to Make Good Decisions: 4 Secrets Backed by Research.* In his post, Eric points to several studies and books that consider the issue of emotions in decision-making, and it turns out that "not only do we need feelings to make decisions, engaging them also leads to better decision." As expected, it's not as simple as just turning to your gut for decision-making. Eric boils it down to this: "Definitely trust your gut on a subject if it's something you're an expert at." If you're still not sure, he offers a clever way to tackle a decision: "Just ask yourself, 'What advice would I give to someone else in this situation?'"

This is where I went wrong. First, I allowed my emotions to completely hijack the process despite my lack of expertise in real estate investing at the time. Second, I failed to think of the situation objectively and ask myself what I would counsel someone else if they asked about the tenant. Stepping back, there is no way I would have advised someone to accept that tenant.

I learned a difficult lesson in 2006: as a landlord you have a responsibility first and foremost to protect yourself. By all means engage in charity work outside of real estate—donate your time, knowledge, and money to worthy causes. But remember that investing is a business. This isn't the time to do someone a favor. Investing in real estate requires a rational analysis of the facts and the numbers. Treat every aspect of investing like a business.

Once you have expertise, you can trust your gut, but if warning bells go off in your head as you're making any financial decision, do yourself a big favor and heed them. The same can be said of any endeavour, whether personal or professional. When in doubt, figure it out. And if you're pregnant, be especially cautious about making purely emotional decisions!

24

ASKING FOR MORE

Gratitude doesn't change the scenery. It merely
washes clean the glass you look through so you
can clearly see the colors.

— UNKNOWN

Several months after Malcolm died, my good friends Ras and
Marilynn called to say they wanted to come spend a weekend
with me to help with my healing. Ras is a Reiki master, and
she was on a mission to use her healing hands to do my battered body
and psyche some good.

They drove several hours to my house, bringing a good supply of red
wine with them. I welcomed their visit. These two ladies have a gift for
making me laugh hard and feel great regardless of the circumstances,
and I was certainly in need of that form of therapy. But I had no intention of letting Ras work during their stay. I didn't want to be a burden.
When Ras pulled out her massage table, I began to resist.

"Ras, I'm fine. You don't need to do this. You didn't come here to work. I'm so happy that you're here—that's enough."

"I know I don't need to do this. It's not work. I *want* to do this for you and for me, too."

"I know, but you really don't need to. Maybe some other time."

This went on for a few minutes before Ras looked at me sternly—or as sternly as she is capable of—and said,

"You need to learn how to receive. You're good at giving, but you're terrible at receiving. It's just as important to receive as it is to give. When someone offers you something or when something good happens to you, here's what I want you to say: 'Thank you, Universe—please give me more!'" Now repeat after me: 'Thank you, Universe—please give me more!'"

I laughed of course, and then, typically, I began to argue with her. You can't do that. It's impolite. You just don't say stuff like that. It's selfish.

Her eyebrows shot up. "Repeat after me. . . ."

Ras won, as she always does, and so did I because I learned a very important lesson that day, one that I've shared with many good friends. We are taught at a young age that it is obnoxious to ask for more when someone gives you something and it is inappropriate to expect more. Be grateful for what you have received and for what you already have. That's enough, right?

Perhaps that's true where social interactions are concerned, but Ras'slarger point is that this is about your relationship with the universe. This is about believing you deserve all the good things in your life, and in fact, you deserve every single thing you desire, provided it does not come at someone else's expense.

Ras wasn't suggesting I vocalize her phrase but instead that I say it to myself and to the universe to make it quite clear that a) I understand I do in fact deserve the goodness that just came my way; and b) I fully expect and deserve more or better in the future. It's about gratitude and expectations all wrapped into one lovely bundle.

FIND THE GOOD, MAKE ROOM FOR MORE

Pick any transformational author and look through their work. They have pretty much all said that before something new can come into your life, you must be grateful for the goodness that's already there. I know it's not always easy to feel grateful when you're facing a lot of darkness in your world, but regardless of where you're at, there is always something good to be found.

After Malcolm died, it took a long time for me to find any bright spots in my life. But we can experience moments of gratitude for the many small gifts that friends, family, and the universe bestow on us daily, even when our world is in turmoil. The more you focus on the good bits, the more they seem to multiply. The more you expect good outcomes, the more they seem to show up.

After nearly ten years of living with cancer and watching my first husband die from it, I had become quite jaded and cynical. It was not an easy process to turn that around, but when I did begin to shift my thoughts and expectations, the results were significant. My life, my business, and my relationships all changed for the better.

Gratitude has played a large role in my personal transformation. Something that Wayne Dyer said has stuck with me throughout the years, "When you change the way you look at things, the things you look at change."

You can choose to feel sorry for yourself and spend time complaining about what's all wrong with your world, but you'll feel rotten, and not much will change. I was an expert at this. I spent a few years after Malcolm died wallowing in self-pity and being mad at myself and the universe for all the garbage I had to deal with. The funny thing is that the more you focus on the garbage, the more garbage you find.

I was a slow learner. I persisted in being negative about my life and my expectations until I finally realized I wasn't getting anywhere. It dawned on me that I had to make a change or face more misery. That's when I began to evaluate my attitude and my expectations.

There was good reason to resist Ras: the act of expecting more and asking for more runs counter to our training. As children we are taught to be grateful. To say we want more is to exhibit signs of selfishness, and no one likes a selfish child. Our programming starts from a young age, particularly for girls. You must be nice. Good girl. You must say "Thank you" when someone gives you a gift, and it's rude to ask for more. Be happy with what you have. It's better to give than to receive, or so the old adage goes.

When I talked to Ras about my hesitation, she pointed out there needs to be a balance between giving and receiving, something which is often difficult for women. We are the care "givers" and not the care "takers." We want to give to others, to help out, to nurture. We are told that the more you give, the more you get, but it doesn't always work out. Ras shared many examples from her own life in which she gave constantly and ended up drained. I could relate. It also wasn't hard to come up with multiple examples from my friends' lives.

Ras reframed the issue for me. "By changing the saying to 'the more I receive, the more I can give,' you keep yourself filled up emotionally, physically, and spiritually." It's not a zero-sum game where if you benefit, someone else loses. It is possible for both people to win. When Ras did her Reiki treatments on me, I felt better, which meant I was in a better position to move forward. She was delighted to be able to help me out. We both won in the process.

THE MORE YOU

RECEIVE, THE MORE

YOU CAN GIVE.

To then turn around and say to the universe, "You know what? I deserve this kind of help, and I want more, please" is not arrogant or selfish. It's simply a recognition that I deserve good things to happen to me. *So do you!* And it's time that we tap into that. The more you receive, the more you can give.

The next time someone offers to do something nice for you, instead of telling them why you won't accept it, say "Thank you," and accept the gift. Then in your head, repeat after Ras, "Thank you, Universe—please give me more."

25

THE BULLY IN YOUR BRAIN

You can't fix a financial problem with money.
You can only fix a financial problem by
changing yourself.

— SUZE ORMAN

Something happened to me in my twenties, and it wasn't good. Of course, it never occurred to me at the time that I was changing in a fundamental way. I was far too busy reacting to my environment.

You already know something of the environment I'm referring to, but perhaps the most insidious change happened internally. Without realizing it, I had acquired the worst kind of bully. This one didn't leave any visible bruises, nor did it yell at me in public. Instead, it worked entirely behind the scenes.

The bully was a voice in my head that shot down every idea I had. Every moment of enthusiasm was tempered by the ever-present naysayer in my brain.

When I look back, I realize the bully developed over a long period of time. For years I was surrounded by key people who were consummate rain-on-your-parade types. If I shared a new goal, they came up with forty ways in which I would fail, couching those doubts in the language of "just being realistic." These prominent, negative influences in my life, coupled with the mental fatigue of constantly dealing with cancer, wore me down to the point that my own enthusiasm disappeared. And that's when the bully showed up.

I no longer needed negative people telling me I couldn't accomplish my goals; I now did it all by myself. Every time a moment of inspiration made it through the fog, my internal bully would pipe up and tell me I was being ridiculous.

Of course, you can't do that—you don't have the resources.

You don't have the time.

You don't have the contacts.

You don't know the first thing about it.

You're not good enough to pull that off.

I doubted myself in every imaginable way and, as a result, my expectations got smaller and smaller.

It took a long time for me to realize that over a period of ten years, I had become a negative person. Not externally, of course. I'm sure if you talked to my friends back then, they would have said that I was a positive person. We can all put on a good show when we need to.

The negativity showed up in the most damaging place—my self-talk. The way I spoke to myself and criticized my every move was appalling. If a friend ever spoke to you the way I spoke to myself back then, you would send them packing. Who needs friends like that?

In his book *10% Happier: How I Tamed the Voice in My Head, Reduced Stress Without Losing My Edge, and Found Self-Help That Actually Works—A True Story*, Dan Harris shares his attempts to tame his own brain bully. He uses meditation to help quell his own tendency to veer into the worst-case scenario at the drop of a hat. He describes some hilarious moments as he worked on mastering meditation. Meditation sounds like it should be easy—sit quietly, breathe in, breathe out, empty your mind, relax—but it's not. However, even if you don't master it, it still works well. Millions worldwide have discovered the benefits of meditation.

Back in my bully days, I didn't know about the beneficial effects of meditation. My approach was different, and I'll share the things that worked for me, but the bottom line is that every person needs to find something that works for them as they deal with internal criticism.

It's also worth noting from Dan's book that this isn't the sort of thing you cure in one epic, meditate-'til-you-bust session. Even if you find relaxation and positivity, you still need to develop a way to deal with the bully who will pop up at the most inconvenient times.

This is what worked to get me out of the negative self-talk rut I fell into after Malcolm's death:

1. VISION BOARD

I know, it's cheesy and so clichéd. Every transformational guru talks about the importance of putting your goals up in pictures in a prominent place so you are constantly reminded of them.

There was something about the process of sitting down with a heap of magazines, though, that really clicked for me. As I thumbed through the pages looking for images that resonated with me, I started to think more and more about what I really want. When I put the images on a poster, they had one of two effects on me: they excited me, or they brought out the bully. It was the appearance of the latter that told me where I needed to do more work.

I have had a vision board for the past twelve years, and it's curious how all of the items on my visual list are getting accomplished one at a time.

2. WRITTEN GOALS

I can't remember who first told me this: Your goals don't count until you write them down in black and white.

Figuring I had nothing to lose, I started to write down my goals. At first I put dates on the goals, but then I'd beat myself up every time I missed a deadline (which happened a lot), so I stopped adding dates. Instead, I started to trust that I would accomplish them at the right time, in the right way. If I found myself procrastinating on a goal, I'd stop to think about why. Sometimes it was the wrong goal, and I'd realize it only after sitting with it for a bit. Other times I met some good-old internal resistance, so I'd tackle those limiting beliefs and move forward.

I continue to keep my top three goals front and center, in writing, to keep me on track. It's easy to become distracted by life. This is a way to remind me of what really matters.

3. EFT (EMOTIONAL FREEDOM TECHNIQUE)

Emotional Freedom Technique, or EFT, works for me, for our thirteen-year-old, who requests it when she's ill or stressed, and for our ten-year-old when she has a nightmare. There's a reason our girls ask for it—they get results with it.

EFT is essentially reflexology for your emotions, except instead of pressing on key pressure points, you tap on them while mentioning the issues you're addressing, following a prescribed(ish) format.

Rather than do a dismal job of explaining it, I will simply refer you to a couple of key resources that I have used to learn more about this approach:

- www.emofree.com—by EFT founder, Gary Craig. He offers a free tutorial to get started.

② www.TheTapping Solution.com—by Nick Ortner. This website has a lot of resources on it as well.

Even if your mind is slammed shut to this option and you're thinking there's no way in hell it will work, give it a try. I used to think the same thing, but after working at it, I've had good results for myself and my children.

4. NATURE

If you're feeling low, get outside. Get some exercise in a place where you can see trees, let the wind play with your hair, and experience nature.

At my lowest points, I would strap on my running shoes and head into the countryside for what I've dubbed pavement-pounding walks with the universe. While it's true I was walking on pavement, I was also surrounded by fields, trees, ponds, cows, and horses—and very little traffic. At night I would pretty much have the place to myself, which is just as well, since most of the time I was speaking to myself.

It's hard to stay miserable when you stare at a beautiful lake or hike on a trail through the woods. For a great look at the science behind nature's influence on your brain, read *Your Brain on Nature* by Eva M. Selhub and Alan C. Logan. Nature has a profoundly therapeutic effect on your brain. The best part is that it's free.

GIRL TIME

One loyal friend is worth ten thousand relatives.

— Euripides

So far I have interviewed more than three dozen women for this book project. While they have all had different experiences of loss or divorce, there is a common thread in their stories: each either did benefit or could have benefitted from close, supportive friendships.

A while ago I had the chance to spend a few days with two girlfriends I hadn't seen in years. I cannot remember the last time I laughed so hard. At one point—true story—as we laughed uproariously over another one of our shared stories, a framed print came crashing off the wall. Most normal people probably wouldn't laugh when a really nice print gets damaged, but that just made us laugh even harder.

I've had the chance to spend a lot of quality time with my girl-friends, and it occurs to me how lucky I am to have such great friends. It reminds me of the words of many of the women I have interviewed.

They talked about the importance of their female support groups as they went through trauma. Their network of girlfriends played a key role in the process of healing and moving forward. Nurturing strong ties with their girlfriends is now a priority.

It's too easy to lose touch with our friends. We have the best of intentions, and we certainly mean to set aside some time to get together but somehow school, work, the yard, extra-curricular sports, and the bustle of life all get in the way. How does time evaporate so quickly?

THE BUSY TRAP

In a great article entitled "The Busy Trap," Tim Kreider makes a persuasive argument for controlling our addiction to being busy. He ends with a fantastic line: "Life is too short to be busy."

What if we all agreed to stop saying we're "crazy busy" when people ask us how we're doing? It's become a bit of a cliché; isn't everybody busy these days? I have yet to hear someone say, "I've got all the time in the world."

I think Tim's on to something. Our grandmothers were crazy busy trying to raise kids with none of the conveniences we have today, yet I doubt they responded with "I'm so busy" when they crossed paths with their neighbors.

My dad put the issue of being busy into perspective. In August of 2014, we began a major renovation on our house. In addition to building a new office for me, we gutted and added several feet to the kitchen. Now that it's done, it looks fantastic, but during the renovation our place was a disaster. We created a temporary, makeshift kitchen in the basement with no stove, no running water, no sink, and no dishwasher. The closest tap was in the laundry room, which is where we hauled the dishes to wash them in the laundry tub. We would then stack rinsed dishes on the washer to dry.

One night during that time, my dad called to say hello.

"How's the renovation going?" he asked.

"It's going well and proceeding on schedule, but man is it tiring. All the extra work of cooking on a hot plate and dragging the dishes to the laundry room is starting to get to me. Every time I want or need water, I have to head to the laundry room and think carefully about how I'm going to clean food. It's a real pain. I know it will be worth it when this is done, but in the meantime, we're not having much fun."

There was a momentary pause.

"You know, when I was a child, I would hitch up the horses to the wagon and head down to the slough to get water in barrels so your grandmother had water for laundry. Our drinking water came from a hand pump in the barn."

My Grandma would have killed for my temporary kitchen with running water in a nearby laundry room complete with a washer and a dryer. Never complain to your parents about being busy. It won't end well. Times were just as busy back in their day, but they didn't wear it as a badge of accomplishment as we do today.

Back to the subject of friends. When Malcolm died, I discovered just how critical friends are. My family lives several provinces away, so they weren't there for the aftermath of loss. It was my friends who stepped in and provided much-needed support. My male friends helped out with computer work, renovating the house, and maintaining the yard until I finally figured out how to do it by myself.

My female friends were my emotional support. They listened to me as I cried, poured the wine, offered words of reassurance and, much later, doled out tough love in a bid to help me move forward.

There's a saying that family is your support through thick and thin. That may be true for some people, but some family dynamics leave a great deal to be desired. Of course, we should all spend time with our extended families and foster those relationships too, assuming they're not the kind of people who make you want to rip out your eyeballs. But the stories of support and strength I've heard through my research are mostly about friends in general, and girlfriends in particular. My friend Bona has a brilliant phrase for the people who form our emotional support system: **the family we choose.** They might well be our biological family members, but more often than not, they include the friends we love dearly.

So if it's been a while since you've had a chance to spend some quality time with your girlfriends, I suggest pulling out the calendar and setting up a date as soon as possible. Stay connected. Your kids will survive, your partner will manage, and your other obligations can wait. Just ensure the art is securely fastened to the walls wherever you meet.

27

LEARNING TO RELEASE

Letting go means to come to the realization
that some people are a part of your history
but not a part of your destiny.

— STEVE MARABOLI

Profound loss brings with it a twisted advantage: it completely changes the way you look at your life and the people in it. I call it an advantage because so many of us float through life on autopilot, never moving beyond superficial analysis. Who has time for deep thoughts, anyway?

The weeks I spent sitting on the floor of my house, mired in loss, gave me time to think. Granted, not at first. For the first few months, I was in shock. Even when the severity of my situation became clear, I still got by in a daze of to-do lists, dropping into bed absolutely spent at the end of each day.

Eventually the fog lifted and, despite the sadness I swear I could feel in my bones, I started to take a good look at every aspect of my life.

Where was I? Why was I there? Who was a part of my life? How did they come to be there? What did I want?

It all boiled down to this: I wanted to be happy. I wanted to feel joy and love and peace and satisfaction. And I wanted to accomplish something significant with my life, to use my abilities to make an impact in some way. I'd had enough negativity and setbacks to last a lifetime.

I came across Jim Rohn's motivational recordings, and they changed the way I looked at myself. One of the first things I heard him say was, "Don't wish it was easier; wish you were better. Don't wish for fewer problems; wish for more skills. Don't wish for less challenge; wish for more wisdom." I interpreted his advice to mean, "Stop whining and find a way forward."

In the process of moving forward, I absorbed another of Jim's nuggets of wisdom: "In five years you will be the average of the people with whom you spend the most time." Look at the people who are exerting influence in your life and ask yourself, "Do they represent the type of person I want to become? Do they inspire me to become a better person in some way, whether professionally or personally? Do they give me energy, or do they bring me down? Do I enjoy their company?"

In the year after Malcolm's death I hardly socialized. Most of the time I sat in my yard or on my sofa staring at nothing in particular and thinking about my life. For the longest time my thoughts were of the "this really sucks" variety until I stopped feeling sorry for myself and started to sort out what I wanted.

When I made a decision to turn things around, I also resolved to spend time only with people who were positive and proactive. By positive I do not mean people who always say life is awesome and couldn't be better, while being one synapse away from a meltdown. I'm talking about the people who really, profoundly have a positive outlook toward life. Sure they moan like everyone else on a bad day, but not for long. Most of the time they are motivated, can-do people.

That posed a big problem: some of the key people in my life were also some of the most negative. When I'd come up with an idea that inspired me, they would think of multiple reasons why I would fail. When the sun was hot and I mentioned how nice it was, they complained that it would probably burn the grass.

When I had a bad day and I turned to them for support, they would respond with, "Yeah, I know exactly how you feel. You wouldn't believe what happened to me." And off they'd go on a lengthy discussion of something nasty they'd experienced, as though we were in a race to the bottom. They would turn the focus of every conversation, regardless of the topic, to them.

Others would make promises and then renege at the last minute. There was always a good excuse—something came up, they were too busy, weren't feeling well, just couldn't manage the time, and so on. They consistently failed to honor their commitments to me.

I started to pay attention to my energy levels. With some of my friends and family, I would walk away from a visit completely energized and happy, while others would leave me reaching for a glass of wine and a comforter.

It became obvious that something needed to change, but how, exactly, do you break up with a family member or with someone you've known forever? The answer, as I discovered, is that you don't.

You simply start distancing yourself and limit your exposure to what I call the energy suckers. If there must be contact, keep it to short, infrequent visits. When the usual patterns of complaints begin, don't engage; instead redirect. When they attempt to inflict guilt, you let it bounce off you, and you keep repeating to yourself, "It's not my issue—it's their issue." When they lash out, hold up a mental stop sign and refuse to allow the nastiness in. Do not accept their dysfunctional approach to life. Learn to lower your expectations of them, and you won't be hurt by their behavior.

It may sound like a calm and balanced approach, but it is bloody hard work. There were times when I had to get away from certain people who sucked the life out of me despite my best efforts to redirect or move to a more positive angle. I just flat out got irritated with those who incessantly rained on my goals. When I was around them, I clammed up and got away as fast as I could. There was no discussion of plans or goals or interests. Forget it. Why go looking for a beating? The same goes for those who promised big things and delivered little.

Here's what I realized: If you spend too much time around crabs who snap at you, they will eventually pull you down to their level and damage you in the process. We get to choose the people who make up our inner circle. As I mentioned earlier, a friend of mine calls it the family you choose. I love that expression. It's your life, your choice. You cannot control where you come from, but you absolutely can control with whom you surround yourself.

You want people who believe in you, love you, appreciate you, support you, treat you well, and who are willing to be honest with you, kindly, when needed. If your family and close friends don't provide that for you, find others who will and limit your exposure to the negative influences, *even if they are your family members*.

As I have said to my daughters over and over again, it is better to spend time alone than to spend it with people who don't treat you in a way that supports you. Set your goals, set your standards, and then choose people whose behavior is congruent with your choices. It will change the way you view yourself and make a big difference in your life.

How will it make a difference? Just imagine yourself running a marathon with an anchor tied to your leg. Now take off the anchor, run the race again, and compare your times. That's pretty much the difference between allowing negative people to hold you back and moving past them to fulfill your true potential.

You choose.

28

THE CHALLENGE OF
REINVENTING YOURSELF

I realized that most people want you to stay
exactly where you are in life—and if you
explicitly talk about how you want more,
they get really uncomfortable.

— RAMIT SETHI

When you undertake growth of any kind, particularly
when it requires significant evolution, something
interesting happens. Some of the people in your life
will surprise you. People who were passing acquaintances or distant
friends will suddenly step to the fore to offer assistance or become
your biggest cheerleaders. Some among your inner circle, from whom
you might expect support, will prove to be your biggest impediments.
It doesn't matter if, like me, the change is the result of trauma or if,
like so many others, you're just ready to make more of your life and
make better use of your skills and abilities. When you seek to change

THE TRICK IS TO NOT LET OTHER PEOPLE'S ISSUES DERAIL YOU FROM YOUR GOALS AND ASPIRATIONS.

something fundamental about your life, the people around you will change too, and the process may be emotionally trying. The trick is to not let other people's issues derail you from your goals and aspirations. This is a touchy subject because it involves speaking openly and even critically about our relationships with close friends and family. I hemmed and hawed about whether to include this chapter given its sensitive nature, but I cannot omit it if I'm to stay true to the point of this book, which is to share what I have learned as a result of my experiences.

This is one of the most potent lessons. It's come up more than a few times in discussions with interviewees. Their comments on the subject were invariably prefaced with, "Between you and me. . . ." Few want to go public with this sort of critical look at key relationships.

The problem with remaining silent about it is that it harms us when we continue to allow other people's issues or judgments to prevent us from moving forward with our lives. Here are a few examples from my own life to serve as illustration.

FOCUSING ON THE NEGATIVE

As the first year of study for my master's degree came to an end, my thesis supervisor called me to his office. I assumed he wanted to discuss my work, so didn't think anything of it. Instead, he informed me the department wanted to offer me a promotion to their PhD program. If I accepted, I would begin the following year as a second-year doctoral student, bypassing the need for a master's thesis. I didn't even know that was possible! You can imagine my elation as I ran home to call everyone I knew to tell them the news. This was a huge opportunity for me! It felt like my fairy godmother had just waved her magic wand and completely transformed my world.

The first person I called, of course, was Malcolm. He was beside himself with joy. "I'm coming right over to celebrate! I'll be there in two hours." Appreciate that Malcolm lived two hours away, so this meant he immediately dropped his work, locked up the shop, drove to his apartment to grab some clothes, and hopped in the car to drive two hours to find me in Montreal.

Then I called a number of people from my inner circle. Most responded exactly as I had hoped—with great joy for me. They were delighted and couldn't wait to connect with me to celebrate. Other responses, however, left me stunned.

"When are you ever going to finish school?"

"How much longer before you get a real job?"

I had a choice. I could focus on all of the positive feedback and words of encouragement, or let a single source of negativity ruin the moment. Back then, I got stuck on the criticism.

By the time Malcolm arrived, I was slumped on the sofa, crying. Some of the most important people in my world just didn't get it. They had dismissed what I was trying to accomplish, what I had accomplished. They seemed more concerned about having me fit it to societal expectations to go to school, get a job, and get on with my life rather than supporting me in my goals.

I accepted the promotion. I protected myself from negative influence by not speaking about my studies or my work with certain people. I realized that to do so would just expose me to more disappointment and negativity, so that part of my world became off-limits in our relationships. They didn't ask, and I didn't volunteer any information.

Many years later, after Malcolm had died, I experienced something similar as I tried to rebuild my life. I had no choice but to reinvent myself, so I figured I would start from scratch and create the life I wanted to have, on my terms. I had walked away from my goals nearly a decade before in order to focus on someone else, but this time it would be different.

In the process of redefining myself, pretty much everything changed. The books I read changed as I sought out people who had transformed their lives in the way I wanted to. My goals became bigger and bolder.

My profession changed; I went from an academic, to a supporter of someone else's business, to a real estate investor. My interests changed. I no longer had time for people who spent their time whining about their circumstances. I had been through enough garbage and didn't want to spend my time listening to people moan without ever taking any steps to change their lives. Sure, I'd sit down with friends, and we'd occasionally complain about a wretched day or something else gone wrong, but it wouldn't last long. We'd get it out of our systems and move on.

When I talked about wanting more or wanting something different for my life, some in my inner circle bristled. "Be grateful for what you have." "You had a great life. Why do you want to change it? Wasn't it good enough for you?" They were uncomfortable with my aspirations and tried to spin it as a rejection of who I had been before Malcolm's death.

THERE IS NOTHING WRONG WITH SHOWING GRATITUDE FOR YOUR LIFE TO DATE AND THEN, IN THE SAME BREATH, EXPRESSING A DESIRE FOR SOMETHING DIFFERENT IN THE FUTURE.

Nothing could be further from the truth. I loved Malcolm and I loved parts of our life together. Now I wanted more. There is nothing wrong with showing gratitude for your life to date and then, in the same breath, expressing a desire for something different in the future. There is no inherent contradiction or, necessarily, a judgment of the past.

I firmly believe we are put on this planet to learn, grow, and contribute.

Without growth of some kind, there is stagnation. No one ever looks at their newborn child and thinks, "I want you to grow up to a certain point and then stop short of your full potential." If other parents are like me, they look at their newborn child and are filled with awe at the gorgeous bundle of potential in their arms and fervently seek every possible opportunity for the child to grow and thrive.

Grow and thrive, not grow to a certain point and be content to count your blessings from then on. For sure, count your blessings—just don't stop there.

ACCEPT CHANGE AND BE GRATEFUL

When I started dating Mark, there was a great deal of resistance from some close quarters. People who had loved and were close to Malcolm knew intellectually I should move on, but emotionally they weren't prepared for it.

Some of my friends were warm and welcoming to Mark despite having been close to Malcolm and not being used to Mark's style. Malcolm had a huge personality and was gregarious in social settings; Mark is quieter, more reserved, and more serious. Malcolm was the politician to Mark's backroom operator, and it proved to be a difficult adjustment for some.

In a moment of complete honesty, one close friend admitted he simply could not accept Mark because it meant admitting Malcolm was gone. He eventually came around to some extent, but our relationship fizzled out in the meantime. I love him dearly, and he still represents an important part of my past, but we have drifted apart and haven't spoken in years. For a while I felt badly about it, but then a wise friend helped me to see that it's normal for people to change. In fact, it's necessary for people to change. That means personal relationships will come and go as a result. The healthiest thing we can do is accept the change and be grateful for the moments we've shared.

When I decided to become a real estate investor, a few people thought I had lost my mind. They didn't tell me this; instead they expressed their concerns to Mark. They did not approve of my career choice. As a result, they never once asked me about my work. To this day there are people in my circle who never speak to me about my work despite its being one of my top passions.

If you ask me what matters most to me, what am I most passionate about, the top two answers would be my immediate family and my mission, of which my work is an expression. My work is a huge deal to me, yet some of the people in my life are simply uninterested. And that's okay—it doesn't have to matter to them. But the scope of the relationship is limited when such an important piece is missing.

I have evolved from real estate investing to helping increase women's financial literacy. There are only a handful of people who really know what I'm up to and how I spend my days. Few know what projects I'm working on, and fewer still know about the various accomplishments along the way.

When I first announced to a few people that I was writing a book, some dismissed it as a trivial project. When you've come from the world of academics but then produce a personal book of this nature, some don't take it seriously.

PEOPLE SAY THE CRAZIEST THINGS

When someone close to you says something regrettable about your goals and aspirations, you have a choice. You can either accept the comment, adding it to your internal baggage—I don't recommend this—or you can let it roll off you and call it what it really is: a reflection of *their* issues, biases, or limitations, not *yours*.

Just to be clear, it's fine to ask questions to seek greater understanding when someone heads in a direction you don't fully comprehend. If a close friend or a family member is simply trying to better understand what you're up to and wants to discuss possible pros and cons, that's great and healthy. But if all they do is rain on your parade or criticize you for your choices, then you need to ask yourself a few questions.

① **What makes them qualified to render judgment? Have they become, done, or acquired what I seek to be, do, or have? If not, why should I take them seriously?**

I recently coached a basketball game in which the opposing coach gave the referee a seriously hard time, questioning every single call or, more often, whining about what the ref purportedly missed.

"That was a travel!!" said the guy as he jumped around on the court. The referee handled it brilliantly. He had obviously been around the block once or twice and encountered this kind of heckling before. "Thank you," was all he ever said back until the coach had danced on the court once too often, and then he was given a warning.

Did the referee buckle under the criticism and the constant nagging? No. Did his confidence take a hit, and did he start to doubt his expertise? No. The coach's comments were treated exactly as they should have been. The referee acknowledged the guy had said something and then promptly ignored his comments. I suggest you do the same with the armchair experts in your life. Thank them for their thoughts and move on.

② **Do they really have my best interests at heart? We assume people try to object to our goals and dreams because they're just looking out for us, but is that really what's going on?**

Most of the time, I give people the benefit of the doubt, assuming they genuinely believe they are trying to be helpful and they mean well, even when they are completely misguided.

However, it may really be about their own insecurities and issues. They don't want you to grow because it makes them feel uncomfortable about themselves. They don't want you to become debt-free and grow your financial wealth because then you won't be in the same boat, and they might have to ask unpleasant questions about their own finances. They don't want you to launch a business and leave the 9–5 job that is killing your soul because it's too scary for them to imagine doing it themselves. If you become a highly successful person on any measure, they may feel inadequate.

Perhaps they haven't made the highest, best use of their skills and passions, maybe they're stuck in a dead-end job that feels mind-numbing, or maybe they feel trapped in debt or a bad relationship or in another scenario that leaves them complaining about their lives. And here you come, trying to move past it all. Instead of wishing you well and encouraging you to progress, they fall into the trap of envy or fear and end up saying discouraging things.

⑤ **Will their opinion make a real difference to me in the end? If my cousin Jack says something moronic about my goal to train for a marathon, will that really matter? Is Jack a runner himself?**

Probably not, or he'd tell you how cool it is that you want to run, too, and offer to run with you on occasion if he can. Is Jack a super-motivated guy who is accomplishing great things with his life? I'm going to go out on a limb here and say that he probably isn't breaking boundaries and racking up accomplishments.

Here's what I've noticed: the people who spend the most time telling me why I can't possibly do or accomplish something are the same people who stay firmly rooted in place in their lives because they are too afraid to commit to change. Have I fallen flat on my face in some endeavors? Absolutely. Do I care? Well, I can't say that failure is fun, but it is important as part of the process of accomplishing any goal. Failure is informative. No one wins or succeeds at anything without first going through a whole lot of failure and learning from the experience.

FAILURE IS INFORMATIVE.

So the next time someone close to you tells you you're going to fail, you can acknowledge that possibly yes, you might fail, but you are going to proceed with the full intention of succeeding. If they have something substantive to say about potential risks or considerations, then it's worth a conversation.

Someone who is genuinely supportive of you will discuss their concerns and nonetheless support you in your decision. They will accept that failure is part of success, and they will help you in any way they can to reach your goals even if they don't share or understand your enthusiasm, because they know that it matters a great deal to you.

And here we have the crux of it: it's not about them—it's about you. Your goals matter to you. Your aspirations matter to you. Your accomplishments matter to you. That's what counts, and not what Jack or Uncle Bob, or Grandpa Joe, or your best friend Sally, or the neighbor behind you has to say about it. You are on this planet to use your skills and abilities in the best possible way. You get to choose your course and your path, not them.

If some of the people in your inner circle continue to cast a shadow on your endeavors, then distance yourself from them as discussed in the previous chapter. Love them, yes, but let go of their issues. They have to resolve their issues, not you. Don't take on their baggage. If someone's reaction disappoints you, find someone who is supportive with whom to share your wins. Focus on the people who get it, not those who don't.

And be deeply grateful for those marvelous souls in your life who *are* loving and supportive.

When all else fails, though, remember the referee's approach: acknowledge the naysayer and walk away, but don't for a moment let their negativity stop you in your pursuits.

29

TAKING THE LEAP

Develop a backbone, not a wishbone.

— Marc and Angel Chernoff

During the summer of 2013, I was approached by a neighbor whom I'll call Mr. Basketball. He asked me if I would consider coaching the girls' competitive Atom team for the area. At first, I thought he was joking, since I was definitely not a basketball coach. The previous two years I had volunteered to help out with my older daughter's Novice house league team, but beyond teaching the bare-bone basics of basketball, I had no experience. I had played for several years, but that was decades ago. Decades, plural.

"You're joking," I replied.

"No, I think you'd do well. I saw you working with the younger girls the other day and you're good with them. I'll help out with some drills and lesson plans from my boys' team; you'll be fine."

"Look, I can barely remember the rules and I'm certainly not qualified to coach."

"You've been doing well with the Novice girls. It's the same idea with Atom girls. We haven't had a team at this level for a couple of years. If you don't do it, there probably won't be a team for the girls. You'll be fine, and as I said, I'll help you out."

No wonder so many people use guilt as a tool. It's effective. I really wanted my daughter to keep playing basketball since it was the only sport she had shown any interest in, and trust me, we had tried the gamut. Against my better judgment, I accepted the gig and promptly went into panic mode. How on earth would I coach this group of eleven- and twelve-year-old girls?

RED RIBBONS

I spent several weeks sweating out my plan, researching plays and drills, until it finally dawned on me that I was going about it all wrong. Every time I've been successful at something, I have done three key things:

⬦ **First, get the head right and the rest will follow.**

⬦ **Second, play to your strengths.**

⬦ **Third, focus on the basics and keep it simple.**

In order to succeed at this, I had to repeat what had worked for me in the past.

Looking back over two and a half decades in business, I realized that every time I failed at an endeavor, the problem started in the six inches of real estate between my ears. The issue wasn't my inability to succeed but that I didn't believe I could. This was true for sports, academics, and business.

To use a basketball example, I once choked in a game because we were up against much taller, older girls with a reputation for being unbeatable. I was intimidated from the moment I stepped on the court.

To this day I remember screwing up a break-away that left my coach shaking his head.

I'd just stolen the ball and easily beaten my opponent into her defensive zone. Instead of flying to the hoop for an easy layup, I stopped short of the basket and screwed up the shot. What the hell? It didn't take much analysis to figure out what happened. I had lost my confidence, which in turn killed my game. My ability hadn't changed, but my performance certainly had. That failure plagued me for years.

Then there's the time that I entered a piano competition against people whom I had consistently beaten in the past. On the day of the competition, I looked over at my main competitor and her teacher, who was highly respected and had a reputation for grooming successful pianists. I started to doubt myself. Suddenly I found myself worrying about the competition rather than focusing on my own piece. To my dismay, I pulled off a mediocre performance of a piece I knew cold and could typically perform very well. Not surprisingly, I came in second.

I could go on with examples from every area of my life, but it all boils down to one thing: when my self-confidence is solid, I perform to the best of my abilities. When I doubt myself or worry that everyone else is so much better, I find myself in a self-fulfilling prophecy.

Two things became clear with respect to my coaching gig. First, I needed to feel confident I could do the job well, and second, I needed to help the girls feel capable and confident from the get-go.

Instead of thinking about all of the reasons I could fail as a coach, I pulled out a sheet of paper and wrote down what was in my favor:

⋄ I've been playing team sports at a reasonably competitive level since I was twelve.

⋄ I understand defensive and offensive strategies.

⋄ I'm competitive.

⋄ I have a research background, so I know how to dig up any information I need.

⋄ I'm motivated to ensure I don't make a complete ass of myself.

⋄ I'm fit, and I know what it takes to get the girls up to game speed.

⋄ Most importantly, I am not afraid to ask for help from more experienced people.

In order to ensure I didn't look like a complete idiot, I reached out to two experienced coaches and asked for pointers. They generously shared their approach as well as the drills they used to reinforce the skills to be mastered. They had both coached teams that had done very well provincially, so their guidance proved invaluable. Why reinvent the wheel? Following the known path to success was fine by me.

Back to my team of Atom girls.

When the tryouts were done, I had a team of twelve girls who had little experience. Not one of them had played at a competitive level. When I set up initial drills to see their basic skills, the results were dismal. They couldn't shoot or dribble, didn't pass, and didn't know how to set up a basic offensive play. They also got tired too easily. What they did have, though, was a great spirit and a desire to learn. That was the glue we needed.

We got to work. The first thing we discussed was the way they behaved and talked to each other. Here's a quick summary of what I said:

⋄ Stand tall with your shoulders back; no slumping.

⋄ We will use only positive, encouraging words when speaking amongst ourselves. Everyone has different abilities and strengths, and we will play to our strengths while improving on our weaknesses.

◇ No complaining about the work to be done. Ever. Success requires effort. If we want to win, then we have to be willing to do the work. If you complain, you do push-ups.

◇ We will never use the words, "I can't." We will instead say, "Yes I can" or ask the question, "How can I?"

◇ First we believe; then we find a way to execute.

◇ We don't just want to practice—we want to practice in the right way. Perfect practice makes perfect execution.

◇ We agree to work hard and do our absolute best at all times. No slacking off.

The phrase "yes you can" quickly turned into "yes we can" as the girls started to gel as a team. Before I knew it, the team cheer became "Yes We Can!" and it stuck for the entire season.

My strategy, beyond getting their confidence up, was simple: if we couldn't initially win with skill, we would at the very least outlast every other team in the league. I began running the girls hard, three times a week, two hours at a go. When the girls complained, they would be rewarded with push-ups. They quickly figured out that complaining was not a winning strategy.

When they protested they couldn't do push-ups, I told them, "You can't yet, but you will be able to soon. You just need practice." At first they couldn't even do five consecutive push-ups, but by the end of the season, they were doing dozens in a two-hour practice.

We worked on their dribbling and passing, and quickly progressed to defensive play. If a team wanted to beat us, they needed to make it to the basket first. Our primary mission was to stop the opposition.

It worked. At the season-opening sort-outs, we surprised everyone by doing much better than expected, which meant moving from a lower division to a mid-level one. That was the good news. The bad news was that we now faced more challenging teams and, consequently, we hit a wall. For the first month and a half, we lost most games quite badly. We kept asking ourselves: What did we do well? What do we need to improve?

The top team in our division beat us by twenty-three points the first time we met early in the season. One month later, we met again, and this time they beat us by only three points. The following month we achieved a break-through by beating them by three points. We continued to exchange wins and losses until the division final at the end of the season. The result? We won the gold medal.

At the end of the season, the girls and their parents presented me and the two assistant coaches, Robb and Carl, with a souvenir book of photos filled with their messages of thanks and appreciation. Front and center was this photo:

I've shared this story because it illustrates my overall message. How many times in life do we let a lack of confidence stop us in our tracks?

How many times do we perform well below our abilities just because we don't think we can achieve a particular goal?

What my group of determined young players demonstrated so beautifully is that we can accomplish great things if we silence our inner demons and take the leap toward a new challenge.

I wasn't a trained basketball coach, yet my two assistant coaches and I pulled off a great year with the help of a few mentors, Professor Google, and twelve girls who were ready and willing to do the work to succeed. We *all* needed to believe it was possible, and we all needed to put in a significant effort to get there.

WHAT MY GROUP OF

DETERMINED YOUNG

PLAYERS DEMONSTRATED SO

BEAUTIFULLY IS THAT WE CAN

ACCOMPLISH GREAT THINGS

IF WE SILENCE OUR INNER

DEMONS AND TAKE THE LEAP

TOWARD A NEW CHALLENGE.

It doesn't matter which goal you choose, nor does it matter if all the chips are stacked against you. It all starts with belief. With a big challenge or small challenge, the process is the same.

But believing isn't enough. The next key step is to take action. All the belief in the world won't do you any good if you never take a step forward. Sometimes that next step seems so frightening that we take the safe way out and hold to the status quo.

When I look back over my life, I can see now there were key moments of decision that led me to where I am today. If I hadn't accepted the dean's offer of a recommendation for a scholarship in my third year of university, I wouldn't have spent a glorious, travel-filled year in France, which also meant that I probably wouldn't have transferred to a university across the country, which in turn meant I wouldn't have met Malcolm.

If I hadn't taken the leap and followed my heart when Malcolm made his overtures in the beginning of our time together, I wouldn't have written this book. Nor would I have met Mark, and the two lovely girls who are the center of my world wouldn't exist.

If, when my neighbor approached me about coaching a girls' basketball team, I had chosen to take the sensible route and avoided looking like an idiot, I wouldn't have had a fun, satisfying year with twelve girls who inspired me, and I would have missed out on a lot of personal growth.

If you've read this chapter and you're thinking, "Yeah right, that's fine for people facing small, insignificant challenges, but my problems are far too big, too serious," I will just say this: in every case there is an open door somewhere.

There were moments from 1998 to 2000 when I wondered if I could continue. The hole I was in was so big and so black, it was overwhelming. I couldn't imagine a way forward.

Yet here I am. There is always a way forward regardless of your circumstances.

It doesn't matter where you have been or what your past looks like. What matters is the choices you make today and every day.

The lessons I've shared are ones I continue to reinforce in my life. I am still learning, evolving, and working hard to survive, thrive, and grow.

You don't get fit by eating sensibly one day, doing a heap of exercise, and then saying, "Well, thank heavens that's done." It requires daily action and commitment. And so it is with success. That's why I regularly ask myself, "Are my actions moving me toward my goals or away from them?" and then I course-correct accordingly.

I still have moments where my inner voice says, "You're a moron," but thankfully I've learned enough to reply, "Maybe, but I'm learning and growing, so get lost, and let me get back to figuring it out."

Every woman can move to a place of joy, security, and fulfillment if she is willing to look honestly at her current situation, make a plan to grow, move forward one step at a time with persistence and determination, and tell the inner critic to get the hell out of the way.

Small steps forward and an occasional big leap.

NO EXCUSES (PLUS AN
ACTION STEPS CHECKLIST)

I have been impressed with the urgency of doing.
Knowing is not enough; we must apply.
Being willing is not enough; we must do.

— LEONARDO DA VINCI

Now that we've gone through the essential elements that need to be addressed, what's your plan from here forward? Nothing will change in your life, nor will you be properly protected, unless you take action.

Information is not what's missing. We've gone through all of the key points, documents, and processes needed to protect yourself financially. The next key step is to do the work. When we procrastinate and make excuses, we show that we do not value the thing we're putting off and, by extension, that we value something else more. It really boils down to choice.

Some may argue they simply can't afford the kind of insurance I've recommended. I'd return that it's only a tiny percentage of the women for whom it's really true. If you can afford cable, you can afford insurance. If you can afford a big-screen television, you can afford to have an updated will in place. If you can go out to dinner, you can afford to save money and pay off debt instead. It's all about choices.

If you tell me you're too busy, I'll tell you that's rubbish. Read Laura Vanderkam's book, *I Know How She Does It: How Successful Women Make the Most of their Time,* to discover exactly how much free time you have. You'll be amazed.

If you tell me bad stuff won't happen to you, I will bang my head against a wall. I don't know if it will, but *neither do you.* Is it really worth the risk? Let me take the liberty of answering that for you—no. No, no, no. It's not worth the risk.

The following is a list of action steps designed to remove the final possible excuse which might be, "*I don't know where to start.*" Start here, and then optimize for your situation as you go along. For an online version of this checklist, visit www.dorisbelland.com/checklist.

ACTION STEPS CHECK LIST

STEP ❶: *COMPLETE YOUR WILL*

Call your lawyer and set up an appointment to write or update your will. Alternatively, sign up for the LegalWills.ca version (or the American or British version if applicable). Use the discount code THRIVE20 to receive a 20% discount.

Set a date to complete it, and write it in your calendar. Do the same for the Power of Attorney documents. No excuses.

STEP ❷: *REVIEW YOUR INSURANCE*

Call your insurance broker and review, increase, or amend your insurance coverage to make certain you are fully protected. This isn't just about covering your mortgage; it's about ensuring you and your children have enough for all of the stuff I covered in *Covering Your Assets*.

For a discussion on why I think mortgage insurance is typically a bad idea, go to my blog post, *"Insurance You Should Ignore."* (http://dorisbelland.com/2013/09/insurance-you-should-ignore/) Set a date by which you will get this done, and write it in your calendar. No excuses.

STEP ③: *DISCUSS FINANCES WITH YOUR SPOUSE*

Now that you're protected in the event of an untimely death, it's time to make a date with your spouse to talk about your finances. Within the next thirty days, sit down, without children around, and take a good look at your current financial state.

This isn't the time to deal with every issue or emergency in your lives. Stick to talking about money. Gather all your financial documents, and sort out where you're at. If you have debts, list them. If you don't understand your statements, turn to someone who can explain them to you. Remember, there is no such thing as a stupid question when you're working on developing your financial literacy. The bottom line is get a snapshot of what you've got (i.e., assets), what you owe (i.e., liabilities), where the information is stored, and how to access it. Be sure to note each other's passwords.

Pay for a babysitter if need be. This is important. You need time, privacy, focus, and quiet to do this well. When the date is booked, set a reminder to do this on a regular basis. No excuses.

STEP ④: *MAKE A PLAN TO TACKLE YOUR DEBTS*

Create a written plan to tackle your debts. Start with your most expensive, unproductive liabilities. If you have credit card debt, then you have a debt problem, and eliminating it should be an immediate priority. Seriously, do not accept paying 18% to 24% to borrow money! Credit card debt must be eliminated first—and then other loans.

STEP ⑤: *GROW YOUR SAVINGS WHILE YOU'RE TACKLING DEBT*

This is where you develop the all-important savings habit while eliminating unproductive debt. Set money aside on a monthly basis even if it is only a trivial sum at first. Saving a small amount is better than nothing, since you're working on developing a good habit. Automate this step to overcome procrastination and resistance. Automation is key to success.

STEP ⑥: *GET THE BIG PICTURE*

Time to draw big picture goals and plans. If your life ended tomorrow, would you be happy with your obituary? If not, what would you like to see written about yourself? "I don't know" is not an acceptable answer. Sit with the idea for a while. Go for walks, meditate, and write in your journal, or pace around your house until you figure it out.

Don't worry about getting it right the first time. Chances are you'll change your mind fourteen times before Sunday. That's fine. Just keep revising this plan until it resonates with you, reflecting your values and your aspirations.

Then place your plan or vision board, if you've made one, somewhere you will see it every day. This is not a document for the filing cabinet—it's a blueprint for your life. Put it where it can inspire you!

Write out the first action step to take. Not fifteen steps, one step. Then get on to it. When you're done, repeat the process. No excuses.

STEP ⑦: *TACKLE INVESTING*

If you've never invested before, today is a great time to start. Take a look at what you've already got (your asset list) and make a plan to move forward based on your goals.

Don't know where to start? Begin with index funds. Here's a quick read that will get you thinking about what to avoid and how to proceed: *The Smartest Investment Book You'll Ever Read* by Daniel R. Solin. Another excellent read that I highly recommend is Tony Robbins' book *Money: Master the Game*. You can also watch for my upcoming workshops on investing.

STEP 8: *BOOK TIME WITH GIRLFRIENDS*

Reach out to them today, and book the date in your calendar. Set a reminder to do this on a regular basis.

STEP 9: *SCHEDULE THINKING TIME*

Set a recurring reminder in your calendar to stop, turn off all electronics, find a quiet spot, and think about your life. This is your regular thinking time to guarantee that you remain on track in your life. Treat it as a non-negotiable item in your calendar, because your life is too important to be put off. No excuses.

I know this can be a pain when you have no clue how to get out of a difficult situation, or when you're so busy you can't squeeze in the time to ask yourself questions about what you'd really like to do, be, or achieve. But you don't want to wait until you're on your deathbed. Trust me, you really can find a way to build in thinking time and significantly improve your life. No excuses.

STEP 10: *CELEBRATE*

As you go through these steps, remember to celebrate. Open your favorite bottle of wine or beer or container of Haagen-Dazs ice-cream, and celebrate the major steps you've just taken to protect yourself. You deserve it.

I would say that now, finally, you're done. But I'd be wrong. This is just the beginning.

I wish you much success and joy.

ACKNOWLEDGMENTS

"You create the future by thanking the past."

— JAMES ALTUCHER

I owe a debt of gratitude to a number of people who inspired and encouraged me along the way.

First and foremost I'd like to thank my husband, Mark. This book would not have been written were it not for his insistence, many years ago, that I put my story in writing. He was also my first test-reader and, while his ebullient responses didn't move my book forward critically, it's precisely that kind of unconditional cheerleading that spurred me to the finish. Given the content of this book, it's ironic that Mark believed in this project long before I did. His unfailing enthusiasm is impressive, especially since the project revolves in large part around my life with another man. I'm lucky he was so patient and persistent all those years ago. Thank you, Universe, for Mark.

Speaking of cheerleaders, thank you to my good friend Wendy Lewis for always being so damned supportive of every project I've undertaken, whether it's this book, my first business with Malcolm, my goal to help grow women's financial literacy, or my real estate investment business. She has read pretty much every word and every blog post I've ever written. That alone qualifies her for an award in tenacity. Love her to bits.

Andrea Lypchuk and Jeff May deserve a special brand of thanks for their ongoing love and support throughout the years, particularly during the hardest moments after Malcolm's death. They raised money for me and were pretty much my emotional life support system in the early days after the funeral. I would have been alone that first awful night were it not for them. I don't know what I would have done without them. They are definitely members of the family I choose.

Thanks to my dear friends Michelle Ganley and Bona Normandeau for their unwavering enthusiasm for, and vocal support of, my book. Their belief in me and my project buoyed me.

I am lucky to be a part of a strong community of female entrepreneurs, many of whom provided valuable feedback when I reached out with questions. Their input helped to frame my thinking on some of the issues I address in this book, and for that I'm grateful.

My thanks to the thousands of readers who have faithfully read my blog over the years and shared their comments. It was their readership in the early days of my blog that made me realize my message resonated with people beyond my inner circle. It's one thing to want to share a story, but it's another thing entirely to confirm an audience for it. Thank you for your encouragement.

Several authors selflessly shared their thoughts, insights, and tips on how to go about publishing my book, and some also served as readers of my early drafts. I'm grateful to Sandra Tisiot, Tammy Plunkett, Lisa Larter, and Gail Vaz-Oxlade, from whom I learned a great deal. Their insights and suggestions made a significant difference.

To the women who were brave enough to share their stories of loss, I extend my profound appreciation. Their experiences and life lessons add an important dimension to this book, and it is all the richer for their inclusion.

Ramit Sethi and Tim Ferriss have no idea how they have inspired and guided me, or at least their blog posts and videos have. They both write as though they are paid by the word, but they are invariably interesting, provocative, and informative. Plus they make me look like a diplomat—I'm looking at you, Ramit—something I always appreciate in a person. My thanks to them for their work.

A shout out to my friend and voracious reader Paige Raymond for her critical feedback on an early manuscript. I benefited from her keen eye for language. Everyone should have a Paige in their life.

I'd like to thank Australia. That's right, I'm thanking an entire continent. You gave me something positive to shoot for at a time when things weren't so rosy in my life, and visiting you continues to stand as one of my goals. I have decided that instead of making it to Australia the conventional way—you know, make plans, buy a ticket, pack two bikinis, and hop on a plane—I'm going to visit when I'm invited to speak. I'll talk on pretty much any subject just as long as the venue is in Australia. Preferably close to a beach. See you soon.

To my great friends Arlene Rasmussen (aka Ras) and Marilynn Wykes, I pass on my profound thanks for their life-changing input. We don't see each other often, but when we do, it's as though time has stood still since our last visit. Their laughter, hugs, and unconditional support of my writing have been invaluable to me. So have their margaritas. I am so glad we met all those years ago trying to sell our wares in the middle of a field. We've come a long way, baby!

Malcolm's father, Ron, is no longer with us, but I feel compelled to note, one last time, how much he meant to me. No one did more to help me through Malcolm's illness and after his death than Ron. The list of things he taught me is too extensive to enumerate and spans the disciplines of construction, literature, art, jazz, and Scotch whiskies, to name but a few. He began as an unapologetic critic of mine and ended up as one of the most cherished people in my life. I miss him and am grateful for the ways in which he enriched my life.

My list of acknowledgments would not be complete without thanking my daughters Annick and Clarice. This has nothing to do with the book, but it has everything to do with me. They continue to teach me important lessons every single year. I am a happier, smarter, wiser, and more patient person because of them. There is nothing I love more than to spend time with them and to hear their laughter. They are my favorite people on the entire planet. Thank heavens Mark got me past my initial reservations about becoming a mother.

Finally, I have two words for Malcolm: thank you. It has been many years since his death, but I still carry his spirit inside me. One thing is certain: without him I wouldn't have learned the lessons that brought me to write this book. He was my first great love and one of my best teachers. I'm lucky to have known him.

ABOUT THE AUTHOR

D oris Belland is a financial literacy educator and real estate investor. She shares her work on women and money through her blog, which has a worldwide readership, and through speaking engagements. She lives in Ottawa, Canada with her family. You can find her blog at www.dorisbelland.com.

Join in the conversation on Facebook:
www.facebook.com/yourfinanciallaunchpad

CPSIA information can be obtained
at www.ICGtesting.com
Printed in the USA
LVOW11s1817160517
534727LV00002B/412/P